A STRANGE THING HAPPENED IN CHERRY HALL

Also by Jasmine Warga

A Rover's Story
The Shape of Thunder
Other Words for Home
Here We Are Now
My Heart and Other Black Holes

A STRANGE THING HAPPENED IN CHERRY HALL

JASMINE WARGA

HARPER
An Imprint of HarperCollins*Publishers*

A Strange Thing Happened in Cherry Hall

For information address HarperCollins Children's Books, a division of HarperCollins Publishers, 195 Broadway, New York, NY 10007.
www.harpercollinschildrens.com

Library of Congress Control Number: 2023948578

ISBN 978-0-06-345026-4

CHILDREN'S FICTION

2 4 6 8 10 9 7 5 3 1

Typography by Julia Tyler

First Edition

Printed and bound in India by Thomson Press India Ltd

For Uncle Moose and Aunt Anna

Ed

Dr. Hale

Rami's Mom

H.F. Bottemtow

Rami

Theodore

Blue

Agatha

Veda

In Which the Turtle Is Introduced and a Painting Is Stolen

Our story might not truly begin with the turtle, but I'm going to start there.

The turtle in question is named Agatha. Her name was given to her by a human who had noticed her existence.

Most humans did not notice her existence.

Agatha is important to our story because she lives in the garden behind the Penelope L. Brooks Museum. In the warmer months, she moves slowly—very slowly; she is, after all, a turtle—nibbling on food left over by picnicking families. (During the summer, the garden behind the Penelope is a very popular picnic spot.)

Occasionally, a human will spot Agatha and clap with delight. But mostly she is left alone.

In the winter, she tunnels underground to hibernate. And to stay away from the cold. Turtles prefer going underground to wearing winter coats.

The day the painting was stolen from the museum was the warmest day that Maple Lake had had so far that year. The sun beamed down on the garden. That heat and goldenness radiated into Agatha's burrow.

A warm, bright wedge of sunlight woke her up.

She crawled (very slowly) out of the burrow. She happened to emerge at just the moment that the robber was scurrying away with the painting.

She saw the culprit.

Agatha noticed many things about the thief. She noticed their height. Their clothes. She noticed how quickly they moved.

Turtles are good at noticing.

But she also noticed that the sun that had felt so warm in her burrow didn't feel quite as warm up here aboveground.

She tucked herself back into her burrow.

She would wait for warmer weather.

In Which There Are Mysterious Marks on the Wall

Rami was staring at the marks when he heard the voice.

The marks were faint against the cream-colored walls. Barely there. A scratch more than anything, really. It looked as though someone had taken a pencil and lightly etched a couple of stray lines.

Rami blinked. When he opened his eyes, he expected the marks to be gone. But they were still there.

Because Rami's mom worked at the museum, he was frequently forced to spend time here. Immediately after the theft occurred, Rami had stayed away from Cherry Hall, the room in the museum where the stolen painting used to hang. But then he worried that the staying away made him seem guilty somehow.

So, he came back to Cherry Hall in the afternoons and just sat. Sometimes he would read his book. Sometimes he would do his homework. But now it was spring break, and he didn't have any homework. And he'd already read his book. Twice.

Which meant that all that was left to do was stare at the wall.

And staring at the wall was really very boring.

Until he noticed the marks. Until he heard the voice.

On this particular day, Cherry Hall was completely empty. Except for Rami, of course. It was Monday afternoon, which meant the museum was closed. And the cleaning crew, which his mother oversaw, had already done their full mop and sweep of the room. The walls had been wiped down and the frames had been dusted.

Everything was sparkling. Even the empty space on the wall where the painting that had been stolen had once hung.

The stolen painting was called *Untitled*. Literally. That was its name. Its name was its lack of name.

Rami thought everything might've been easier if the stolen painting had a proper name.

While he stared at the mysterious marks on the

wall, he thought about the missing painting's lack of a name. He tried to come up with a title for it, but he couldn't think of anything good.

It was then that he heard the voice.

At first, he stayed very still.

But then he heard it again. This prompted him to stand up from the bench where he had been sitting.

He looked over his shoulder. He didn't see anyone. He looked to the side. He still didn't see anyone. He was convinced that he was alone.

(He wasn't alone. But he would figure that out soon enough.)

Rami moved closer to the wall.

He reached out instinctively and then quickly withdrew his hand, remembering the paramount rule of art museums. No touching.

This was a rule his mother had reminded him of over and over again.

"We're lucky they let me bring you to work," she'd said. "But you need to behave. Be quiet. And absolutely do not, under any circumstances, touch anything."

Rami had thought it would be a whole lot luckier if he was allowed to stay at home. By himself. Like all the almost-twelve-year-olds that he knew. But his mother was a worrier. When he asked her about it, she would say, "You can't blame me for being a worrier. I was born in a war zone."

"Maple Lake isn't a war zone," Rami would answer.

"That's why your father and I came here," Rami's mom inevitably would reply. "Because we wanted you to have a better life in a safe place."

"Maple Lake is safe," Rami would say. The conversation always had this circular nature. His mother explaining that they came to Maple Lake because it was safe, Rami agreeing that Maple Lake was safe, and then Rami asking to stay home alone because of the aforementioned safeness. But he never got anywhere.

Which was why he was here on this particular afternoon. In Cherry Hall. In the Penelope L. Brooks Museum, which everyone in Maple Lake simply referred to as the Penelope.

No one in Maple Lake had cared much about the Penelope. Until two weeks ago. When the painting went missing. Now the Penelope was all anyone wanted to talk about.

"Hello?" Rami heard the voice say.

The voice was quiet at first.

Scarcely audible.

Rami spun around.

He still didn't see anything. Not yet. But he was getting closer.

"Hello?" the voice said again.

He glanced back at the wall. And it was there, on the wall, that he first saw her shadow. This time, when he turned around, he saw a girl.

The Floating Girl

The girl was probably around his age. Maybe a little younger. Maybe a little older. It was hard to tell. Rami straightened his spine. If she was trying to determine his age, he wanted her to guess on the older side. He pushed his curly dark hair away from his face. He put on his most adult-looking expression.

"Hello," the girl said a third time. "Can you see me?"

She was pale white with a freckled face and long, thick dark brown hair that almost reached her waist. Her hair had that static-shock quality, puffing out around her, like it was raising its hand, waiting to be called on. She had big green eyes that blinked rapidly. And was wearing a blue dress that seemed like something someone would wear in summer instead of winter. Not that Rami knew much about fashion.

In his mind he replayed what the girl had said: *Hello. Can you see me?*

Can you see me? Rami was puzzled. It was such a strange thing to say. He figured he must've not heard her correctly.

Sometimes Rami felt that way, though. In the crowded hallway at school. In the cafeteria when he scanned for a familiar face that wasn't one of the faces he'd known since kindergarten. Those friends had decided, just this year, right at the start of school, that they didn't want anything to do with him anymore.

Can you see me? Rami repeated in his head, before he said aloud, "Uh."

"Uh?" she said.

Rami wondered if he was imagining the girl.

Rami wondered a lot.

Rami swallowed.

(As of recently, he swallowed a lot, too.)

He looked down at his black sneakers with the orange stripes on the sides. His mom had bought them for him as a present before the start of sixth grade. That was back when he'd thought middle school was going to be way better than it had turned out to be so far. The shoes felt a bit too tight now, but Rami wasn't ready to get rid of them.

"Can you please let me know if you can actually see me?"

Rami flipped his eyes back up to the girl. "Yes. I mean, yeah. I mean, why wouldn't I be able to see you?"

The girl let out one of the loudest sighs that Rami had ever heard. It sounded almost like a train whistle. Rami jumped and then tried to pretend like he hadn't. (He wasn't fooling anyone.)

"Don't be so loud. The guard is going to come," Rami said.

The Penelope had two security guards on its payroll, but only one guard worked at a time. If you were looking to blame something or someone for the robbery, the fact that there was only ever one guard on duty seemed like a good place to start. But in fairness, the Penelope was a small museum. And there were cameras in every room. (The cameras had not proven helpful, but we will talk more about that later.)

"It won't matter in the slightest if the guard does come," the girl answered. "The guards do not see me. I've been trying to talk with them for days."

The girl didn't speak like most of the kids he

knew from school. And there was a lilting quality to her voice. It reminded Rami of something from an old movie.

It was then that Rami noticed the girl's feet. She wasn't wearing any shoes. Which would've been strange enough on its own, but upon second glance, it was obvious that her feet were not touching the floor.

She was floating.

Barely.

But she was floating.

Rami screamed. Quickly, he covered his mouth with his hands. He couldn't believe that he'd screamed. That was really very embarrassing.

But then he looked back at the girl's floating feet and felt like screaming all over again.

His skin was hot and rashy. He held his breath for a long time.

The girl flashed a toothy smile at him. "No need to be frightened. But where were we? You were speaking about the security guard?"

Rami kept his hands over his mouth. He shook his head very fast. The room seemed like it was spinning. He couldn't stop looking at the girl's floating feet.

He was sure he was imagining them.

He had to have been, right?

Squeezing his eyes very tight, he shook his head again.

"Is everything okay?" a gruff voice asked.

Rami opened his eyes.

The security guard stood in the archway entrance of Cherry Hall. He was eyeing Rami suspiciously. This was exactly what Rami did not need.

"I'm o-okay," he managed to stammer.

The security guard, whose name was Ed, frowned. He stared at Rami for a long time. Sweat pooled at the back of Rami's neck.

Ed made a humph-ing sound, and his frown deepened. Rami knew for a fact that this security guard was not a fan of his. He hadn't liked Rami being here even before the painting went missing.

"This isn't a day care," Ed had said to Rami's mother more than once.

And now that the painting had gone missing—let's just say Ed was convinced Rami had something to do with it.

"If you're okay, why did you scream?"

"I . . ." Rami's mind went blank.

"Just know that I'm watching you." Ed made the

universal sign with two fingers for "I'm keeping tabs on you." Rami wasn't sure why Ed had felt the need to say the warning and then act it out, but he nodded and forced his face to look very serious.

"I promise—"

"I don't need your promises. I'm going to catch you next time."

"There won't be a next time," Rami said, and then quickly added, "Not that there was a first time."

Ed raised an eyebrow, his mouth still set in a downturned line.

After what felt like forever, Ed eventually ambled into another room. Rami took a couple of deep breaths.

"Well, that was strange," the girl said, floating back into view. "Is he always in such a bad mood?"

Rami felt like screaming again. But he didn't.

He had so many questions. Like why was she floating? And why was she dressed for summer when it had been snowy all week?

But he didn't ask any of those questions.

Instead, he said, "Who are you?"

"I promise I'm not pulling your leg when I tell you that I truly haven't the faintest clue who I am," the girl said. "Which is quite the elephant-sized problem, if you know what I mean."

He tried not to stare at her floating feet. But he couldn't stop himself. Hovering just above the museum's shiny wooden floor, they were so pale that they were almost translucent.

"You're floating," he said.

She looked down at her feet. "Oh. Yes. That."

He shook his head once more. Thinking that maybe if he shook it enough, something would shift in his brain to make this all seem less strange. "People don't float. It doesn't make any sense."

The girl shrugged. "I do."

"I asked who you—"

"And as I've already told you, I simply don't know."

"You don't know who you are?"

She blinked rapidly, and then her face moved into a sullen, sour expression. "No. I do not."

"That doesn't make any—"

"Sense?" She finished his sentence for him. "You keep saying that. Repeating things can be quite tedious, don't you think?"

Rami was quiet for a moment. "Uh, yeah, I guess, but what else is there to say? It *doesn't* make any sense. How can you not know who you are?"

The girl who was floating smiled a little. But her smile seemed sad. Rami knew all about sad smiles.

"Well, we are not going to get anywhere if we keep repeating ourselves. Can we at least agree to that?" the girl said.

Rami scratched the back of his neck. His skin still felt hot and rashy. "I guess."

"No. You need to agree. Affirmatively. We must agree to both try harder," the girl said. She moved—or, rather, she floated—closer to him. "Because, you see, I am in dire need of your help."

In Which Rami Realizes the Girl Looks Familiar

Rami looked over his shoulder. He was certain Ed was going to walk back into Cherry Hall at any moment. Also, he was half convinced that the girl must have been talking to someone else.

Given how terribly his sixth-grade year was going, Rami Ahmed didn't think he was in the position to be able to help anyone.

(He was wrong.)

"I'm quite taken with this one," the girl said. She was pointing at the largest painting in the room. It was of a sailboat.

Rami had always thought that painting was kind of boring. He was also confused about why someone would choose to paint a boat on the shore. Wasn't the whole point of boats that they floated on water? Why would anyone care about a boat if it was on land?

He knew he should say something about the painting, but he couldn't think of anything smart. Or nice. So instead, he asked, "You really don't know what your name is?"

"I really don't. I know that doesn't make any sense, but it is what it is."

"You told me to stop saying that it doesn't make sense."

"Actually, I did not. I only commented that you were frequently repeating it. It was merely an observation."

Rami flinched a bit, something that had been happening a lot since the start of the school year, but felt a flush of relief when he saw she was smiling. It was then that he noticed something about her.

Or, rather, he realized that she looked familiar.

"This is going to sound weird," he said.

"But let me guess, you're going to go ahead and blurt it out anyway."

"Probably. Yeah."

"Okay. Well, get on with it, then."

"I think we've met before," Rami said, his voice wavering a bit.

The girl puckered her lips. "Is that so? Then do

you happen to know what my name is?"

Rami shook his head.

"Where did we meet?"

"I don't know."

"Hmm." The girl drifted in the direction of the sailboat painting. "That's not very helpful."

"Yeah. I know. But—" Rami focused on the empty spot on the back left wall. The spot where *Untitled* used to hang.

"You're the girl from the painting," Rami said.

The girl turned her attention back to Rami. It was her green eyes that he recognized the most. In the painting, they weren't blinking. In the painting, they were wide open, drawn to look right at you. Rami didn't know how the artist had done that.

But he liked how, because of the way the girl's eyes were drawn, it felt like he wasn't just looking at the painting, but the painting was looking at him, too.

In the weeks after his former friends had decided he could no longer eat lunch with them, he'd sat in front of that painting a lot. Those memories had come back to him the instant he'd heard the painting had been stolen. He'd missed the painting in a way he hadn't expected.

"You're definitely her," he finally said.

"What are you talking about?" another voice said.

It was not the floating girl's voice. It was his mother's.

"Um," Rami said. He swallowed. Again.

His mother was dressed in her work uniform, a drab gray button-down shirt and baggy scrubs pants. Her curly black hair was pulled into a braid. She looked tired, but she was smiling at him.

"I'm sorry," he said.

"For what?"

He shrugged. There were so many possible answers to that question, but he couldn't find the right words to express any of it.

His mom walked over to him and ruffled his hair. She smelled like she always did after work, chemical and antiseptic with the faintest hint of artificial pine. He groaned and moved away from her.

"You shouldn't say sorry when you're not actually sorry," his mom said.

"I just meant I know you want me to be quiet when I'm here."

"It's okay, habibi." Habibi meant "sweetheart" in Arabic. His mother spoke fluent Arabic, but Rami didn't. But he knew what habibi meant because his mom had been calling him that his whole life.

Rami's mother was born in Lebanon. So was his father. They'd moved to America together when they turned eighteen. His mom always said that they'd come to America searching for something—a better life, bigger dreams. Rami wasn't sure she'd ever found it. But he didn't like to think too much about that.

"Mom—" he started, but then saw she was looking around Cherry Hall. He watched her eyes linger on the spot where the missing painting had once been on display. Rami thought he saw something cross her face. A flicker of understanding. He wondered for a moment if she had seen the floating girl, too.

He was about to ask, when she said, "But who were you talking to?"

"Uh," he said. "No one." He glanced down at his too-tight shoes.

"But you were talking."

"No, I wasn't," he insisted.

He looked around, searching the room for the girl. But she was no longer there. Maybe she'd never been there at all.

A Pizza Dinner and a Knock at the Door

Rami took a bite of the delivery pizza. Usually, his mom said that pizza was too unhealthy and too expensive, which made it a double no. But she'd surprised him tonight.

"It's your vacation," she'd said. "We should do something fun."

It was the Monday of spring break. They were three days in. He wasn't sure why his mom had decided to mark the occasion now, but he wasn't going to argue with her.

After all, he wanted pizza.

"Thanks for getting pizza," Rami said. The moment it was out of his mouth, it sounded wrong and too formal. Rami hung his head and then snuck a quick glance at the empty chair across from him.

Until a few months ago, that empty chair had never bothered Rami. He hadn't even thought of it as empty. His dad had left before Rami turned two, meaning he had zero actual memories of the guy. For as long as he could remember, it had always been just him and his mom. And that was fine. That was more than fine.

When he was five, his mom told him that the last she'd heard, his dad was in Atlanta. She said they didn't keep in touch. Rami hadn't thought to ask any more questions after that.

But one afternoon this past December, on a particularly cold day when Rami was feeling upset about everything that was happening at school, he got curious and started poking around in his mom's room.

At first, he found only things he expected—her sketch pad, several used charcoal pencils, books about birds and robots and aliens. But then he found what he now thought of as the Photo.

In the Photo, a baby is being held by a guy with a large mustache. Rami's mother has her arms around this guy's neck. Mustached guy has the exact same eyes as Rami, which led Rami to conclude that he was probably his dad.

The Photo brought up a lot of questions for Rami.

Namely, why did his dad leave? They all looked so happy in the picture. His mother's smile was particularly hard to look at. It was wide and bright and carefree in a way Rami wasn't used to seeing.

Rami also wondered about the mustache. He wondered about the mustache a lot. And if he'd ever grow one like the guy he presumed was his dad. And whether or not he'd be able to pull off that look. And if he did, maybe Henry and Matty would let him sit with them again at lunch. (He also frequently wondered if things would be better for him socially if his name ended with a *y* instead of an *i*.)

He'd taken the photo and hidden it under his bed. He kept waiting for his mom to ask him about it, but she didn't. And then he kept thinking he should ask her about it, but whenever he tried, he ended up swallowing down his questions at the very last minute.

And then the painting was stolen, and Rami felt more uncomfortable admitting that (a) he'd been snooping around in her stuff and (b) he'd taken the Photo. He didn't want to look like a thief.

"So, I spoke with Dr. Hale this afternoon," his mom said, jerking Rami back to the present.

Dr. Hale was the bespectacled director of the Penelope. She had curly gray hair and was almost always wearing a checkered blazer and shiny brown leather loafers. She had that accent that most rich people do, where it's impossible to know where they are originally from, but you know that they are fancy and well educated.

Rami chewed his pizza. The gooey cheese took on a metallic flavor as he waited for his mom to say more.

"She says they haven't made any progress in the investigation." His mom set down her fork, and then her knife. She looked straight at Rami. "Which isn't great news."

"She knows you had nothing to do with it, right?" Rami took another large bite even though the metallic taste hadn't gone away. He closed his eyes for a brief second. He pictured the gooey and greasy and delicious cheese. He willed his taste buds to cooperate.

They didn't.

His mom shook her head. "I don't know. I don't think she really believes I had anything to do with it, but she needs to consider all the possibilities. She's under a lot of pressure to recover the painting."

"Did they ever figure out what went wrong with the cameras?" Rami thought about the girl he had seen today. The floating girl. The disappearing girl.

His mother pursed her lips. "There was nothing wrong with the cameras."

Rami gulped down some water. That was really bad news. The cameras had been turned off. And the only people in the museum that day had been the cleaning crew, Ed, and Rami himself. "Did Dr. Hale say anything about seeing anyone else that afternoon? Like maybe a girl? Is there a girl in the video footage?"

His mother leaned back in her chair. She arched her eyebrows. "Why would you say that?"

"I just . . ." Rami faltered. He reached for his water again. "I don't know—someone else had to have been there, right? Besides you and your crew and Ed."

"And you," his mom said.

Rami felt his face turn hot. "Yeah, and me. But you know—"

His mom gave him the most typical mom smile. "I'm only teasing."

"Mom, I'm not joking. There probably was someone else there, right?" Rami insisted. "There had to be. And that someone is probably the someone who turned off the cameras."

His mom smiled wider. But it didn't look anything like the smile from the Photo. "Yes. That someone is probably the someone," she said.

"I know how I sound, but—"

"I know you want to help, but really, I don't want you to worry," she said.

Rami looked down at his plate of half-eaten pizza.

"Are you sure no one saw a girl?" he asked again.

His mom tilted her head. Her eyes narrowed. Her eyes were darker than Rami's and mustached guy's, and moon-shaped. Rami had the mustached guy's eyes—sharp and angular, flecked with gold.

"Rami, habibi, why do you keep asking about a girl? Do you know something? If you know something, you need to tell me right now."

He debated for a moment. He could try to tell his mom. His mom was understanding. She always listened to him.

I think I saw the girl from the missing painting, he could say.

Or *I saw a girl today in Cherry Hall. But I'm maybe the only one who can see her.*

Or he could say *None of my friends will sit with me at lunch. I don't know why they don't want to be friends anymore. Middle school has been terrible. Is there something wrong with me? Is that why my dad left? And also, is my dad the guy with the mustache?*

But he didn't say any of that.

"Never mind. I don't know anything." He kept staring at his uneaten pizza. "I just want them to find the painting."

"Me too," his mom said. And then she repeated, "Me too."

"What if they don't?"

"If they don't?"

"If they don't find the painting," Rami said.

His mom shook her head. "It won't be good."

She didn't elaborate, but Rami had no trouble imagining what "not good" was. Why was it always easier to envision bad scenarios than good ones?

He was thinking about all of this while he helped his mother wash the dinner dishes. The knock on the door came when he was finishing drying his plate. It was a single knock. Loud and purposeful.

Rami's mother looked down at her watch. "It's late. Who do you think that could be?"

"No idea," Rami said, staring at the door.

A Surprise Visitor

Another knock. Equally as loud as the first, but perhaps more purposeful.

Rami held his breath as his mother walked to the door, her feet making indents on the beige-colored carpet.

"Oh, hello, Theodore," his mother said, pulling the door open a bit wider.

Rami gulped. Theodore D. Cornell lived in apartment 1B, directly below Rami and his mother. Theodore also worked at the Penelope. He was the second security guard. But he was not on duty the day that the painting had gone missing, which meant that while he was being questioned, there was less pressure on him than there was on Ed or Rami's mother.

Theodore had actually worked at the museum for

years before Rami's mother started there. It was from Theodore that she'd initially learned about the opening on the cleaning crew, and later, after a few years of work, had been promoted to be the cleaning crew supervisor.

"Rami," his mother called out. "Come say hello to Theodore."

Rami reluctantly walked toward the doorway. He didn't know Theodore very well. He'd only had the briefest interactions with him over the years—slight waves in the hallway, awkward small conversations when his mother sent him downstairs with a plate of leftover food, and every so often a nod or two when Rami crossed paths with Theodore while he was working at the Penelope.

Rami's mother was always encouraging him to be more friendly with Theodore.

"I think he's lonely," she would say.

Rami wasn't sure what to do with that.

Maybe Theodore was lonely. But sometimes people just wanted to be left alone. And Theodore definitely gave off those vibes.

"This was accidentally delivered to me," Theodore said. He held out the latest issue of the *Maple Lake Ledger.*

Rami's heart pounded. Ever since the painting had gone missing, he'd secretly been reading his mom's copy of the *Maple Lake Ledger* every night, as the paper was running an investigative series about the crime.

"Oh," his mom said brightly. She took the newspaper from Theodore. "Thank you."

"You must be one of their only subscribers left," Theodore said, shifting his weight from his right foot to his left. He was a large man who stood with a slight hunch, almost as though he was embarrassed by his immense height. He had a mostly gray beard that still had patches of the rust color that his hair once was. Rami was used to seeing Theodore in his security guard uniform, but tonight he was in plain clothes, which made him look older somehow.

And maybe even more lonely.

"I like their crosswords," Rami's mom said lightly.

"Hmm . . ." Theodore exhaled loudly. He rubbed the back of his neck like he was debating whether to say anything else. "Have you read what they've been writing about the case?"

"Yes, I have, but you know it's just the usual basic stuff. They aren't revealing any new information," Rami's mother answered.

Theodore's eyes settled briefly on Rami, searching him like they were asking a question. Something lurched inside Rami. Did Theodore know about the floating girl? Should Rami say something? Rami held Theodore's gaze for a while before finally looking away.

"Well, it's late. I'm sorry to have bothered you. I just got home, and that's when I saw the paper had been delivered to me instead of you. And so . . ." Theodore trailed off.

"No apologies necessary," Rami's mother said. "Would you like to come in and have some pizza? We have leftovers."

There was a long pause, but Rami was relieved when Theodore shook his head.

"Thank you for the invitation, though," he said. "It's just been a long day."

"I know," Rami's mother said, and Rami could hear the tiredness in her voice, too. "This whole thing is such an ordeal, huh? I really hope the authorities figure it all out soon."

Theodore coughed, looking at Rami again. And then he nodded. "Me too. It's a big mess, that's for sure."

"Have you heard anything else about what

happened with the cameras?" Rami blurted out.

Theodore's eyebrows knitted together. "No. Should I have? Did Ed have new information today?"

Rami's mother laughed awkwardly. She waved her hands in the air. "Sorry about that. You have to understand that Rami is concerned about the painting. Like we all are. He wants to be helpful."

Theodore gave Rami another long knowing glance. Rami's insides shivered.

"I understand. I'm sure the painting will be recovered soon, though," Theodore said after another long pause. "Good night."

Rami only exhaled once his mother had closed the door.

Our Sleepy Turtle Sees the Floating Girl

Another sunny day.

Agatha the turtle poked her head aboveground.

In the window of the museum, she saw a girl.

Agatha knew this was strange because it was early morning, and the museum was not yet open.

Humans think that turtles don't understand things like time and schedules.

Humans are wrong.

Agatha looked at the girl. She wondered what the girl was doing in the museum at this hour.

But then she felt the sun bake down on her head. She knew it would feel warm on her shell. But not warm enough.

She went back down underground.

The Newspaper Borrower

Later that night, after Rami heard the click of his mother's bedroom light, Rami knew he was free to read about the missing painting.

Privacy was not very easy to come by in apartment 2B. There were only four main areas—his mother's bedroom; his bedroom; the kitchen and living room, which were sort of the same space; and the bathroom.

So, Rami only read the *Maple Lake Ledger* at night. When he was certain that his mother had gone to bed.

He would tiptoe out into the kitchen that was also the living room, snatch the most recent copy of the *Maple Lake Ledger*, and then tiptoe back to his room. His mom might've told Theodore that she was only interested in the crosswords, but Rami knew she also read the articles about the investigation.

(And Rami also liked the crosswords. He would often erase his mom's work and try on his own once he knew she was done.)

Rami opened the paper to read today's article. As usual, they had printed a picture of the missing painting. It didn't look exactly like the painting had when it had hung in the museum. Which Rami knew was a strange observation to make.

But paintings look different in person. When you are in the room with them, you can see the texture of the paint. You can get a sense of the painting's size. You can feel the energy of the painting.

(Paintings really do have energy. If you don't believe me, go to a museum and stand in front of one. If you pay enough attention, you'll be able to get a read on the painting's energy.)

Anyway, the picture of *Untitled* was nothing like seeing *Untitled* in person.

But it was good enough for now.

Rami's eyes widened as he studied the picture of the painting. He'd been right.

The girl in *Untitled* was undeniably the same girl he had seen that afternoon in Cherry Hall.

Or maybe not undeniably. The start of middle

school had made Rami feel not so sure about anything. Meaning Rami wasn't confident that he'd ever be certain enough about anything to use the word "undeniably."

But the girl—the floating girl—sure looked a whole lot like the painting girl.

Very close to undeniably so.

In the painting, the girl is standing under a large apple tree. The sky is the best part of the painting. A hazy and brilliant kaleidoscope of golden pink and deep orange hues. Back before the painting went missing, Rami would often stare and stare at the sky. It was easy to lose yourself in it.

The apple tree was the next main component of the painting. It was large in scale compared to everything else. So large, in fact, that it made the girl seem very small. She was easy to miss.

Rami focused on the girl's green eyes. The ones he had recognized. The ones that when they looked out at you from the painting, you felt less alone.

"Who are you?" he whispered. "And what are you looking at?"

Some (Important) Facts About *Untitled*

Before *Untitled* had been stolen, not much had been known about H. F. Bottemtow, the artist who made the painting. After *Untitled* was stolen, the public at large was eager to learn more about the relatively unknown artist. (People tend to be very interested in objects once they go missing, even if they never cared about them before.)

Here are some facts that were uncovered:

H. F. stood for Hannah Frances. Hannah Frances had been born and raised in the Maple Lake area. Her family owned an apple tree orchard. They sold their apples and also welcomed tourists to pick apples in the fall and take hay wagon ride tours of the grounds.

Untitled was the only one of H. F.'s paintings owned by the Penelope. She was considered a very minor artist, but museums in the Chicago, New York, and Dallas areas also had acquired her artwork. She was known for her realistic but dreamy style. When Rami had read that, he'd felt validated. He'd always thought the sky in the painting seemed both like it really existed and also like it had come from a dream world.

No art historians seemed to know much about *Untitled.* They did not know who the girl in the painting was or why H. F. Bottemtow had chosen to paint her.

H. F. Bottemtow was an intensely private person. Not much was able to be discovered about her life, outside of basic details. In the wake of the theft, investigative journalists learned that H. F. Bottemtow had spent time teaching art at various small universities across the country. She had also worked as a grocery store cashier, a dog walker, and a nanny. This struck Rami as odd, but what did he know? Maybe it was common for artists to have several jobs.

The consensus seemed to be that H. F. Bottemtow currently resided at Evergreen Pines, an assisted nursing and retirement facility at the edge of Maple Lake. Evergreen Pines gave this statement to the media: We do not comment on the status of our residents, as privacy is paramount.

Evergreen Pines forbade any media from entering the premises.

Several journalists tried to sneak into Evergreen Pines. They were escorted out by security guards.

There were no recent pictures of H. F. Bottemtow. The only one the paper had managed to dig up was from a long time ago. It showed a thin woman with short dark hair. She was wearing an oversized sweater, and she was turned away from the camera. She had perfect posture. There was a lot of debate about whether this was even H. F. Bottemtow.

When the painting went missing, a statement was released saying that H. F. Bottemtow hoped the painting would be recovered but did not have any further comment on the matter. The fact that she did not have any further comment on the matter just made people want more comments. She didn't offer them.

More journalists tried to sneak into Evergreen Pines. They continued to be unsuccessful.

Rami looked once more at the picture of *Untitled*. He looked at the photograph of H. F. Bottemtow. He tried to remember exactly what the floating girl had looked like.

"You all fit together," he said. "I just have to figure out how."

He briefly imagined solving the case. He imagined an article being written in the *Maple Lake Ledger* about him and the integral role he'd played in finding the painting. He imagined Henry and Matty seeing all the attention he was getting and inviting him back to the lunch table. He pictured himself playing at the arcade for Matty's birthday, entering his initials for the high-score leaderboard.

And then he squeezed his eyes shut and imagined the mustached guy from the Photo hearing about Rami's heroic efforts to solve the case. He imagined his mom smiling that same smile from the Photo.

Rami Ahmed was going to find this painting.

In Which the Floating Girl Scratches the Wall

The girl wandered all around the museum, but whenever she tried to leave, she ended up right back in Cherry Hall. Floating in front of that blank white space.

She'd overheard enough conversations to understand that a painting once hung in front of that blank white space. And that the painting had been stolen.

This intrigued her.

But it was hard to find anything too intriguing when you were literally stuck in an art museum.

And when you didn't understand why you were stuck. Or who you were. Or how long you were going to be stuck.

"Hello, hello," she said again and again to the shorter security guard. The one named Ed.

He didn't respond at all. She floated close enough to him to tap his nose. He shivered and sneezed, but still didn't see her.

Sometimes she played jokes like that. She would blow off his hat. This tended to make him angry. And that was kind of funny.

But other times, she felt closer to crying. She'd get very close to his face and say, "Please help me."

He would still only sneeze.

She thought these actions didn't reflect that well on his powers of observation. No wonder a painting had gone missing.

The other security guard's eyes widened when he saw her. The taller one. The one she'd recently learned was named Theodore.

There was something about Theodore that she recognized. She didn't know why. But she sensed that he felt it, too.

"Hello?" she had said, floating close to him.

His face had drained of color. He'd covered his eyes like a child playing peekaboo.

"You see me, don't you?" she asked. "Please talk to me."

But he didn't. He stood up from his desk and darted down the hallway. She chased him, but when he exited the museum, she wasn't able to follow.

One day, before she met Rami in Cherry Hall, she floated down the hallway. Through the hallway window, she was able to see the museum's back garden. It was then that she saw the head of a turtle poking out.

"Turtle," she said.

The turtle did not say anything. (Of course not. Turtles do not speak the language of humans.) But the girl could see in the turtle's beady brown eyes that this turtle saw her.

"You can see me," she said. "I'm real."

The turtle disappeared back underground. The girl stared out the window, hoping the turtle would come back. It did not.

But the turtle had given her a small gift. A feeling of realness. She held on tight to it. And she longed to feel more if it.

That's why she had scratched at the wall.

She was a little bit ashamed of this act. Did she want to be the type of girl who clawed at the wall while howling in the middle of a museum?

No.

But she also hadn't particularly wanted to find herself trapped in a museum with no knowledge of who she was or why she was there.

After she made her marks, she waited. For someone to notice them. To notice her.

She watched as cleaners scrubbed the floor. Dusted the walls. Adjusted and polished the frames. None of them stopped to notice the marks.

But the boy, as you already know, did.

The boy saw her.

The boy talked to her!

(She did not yet know that the boy's name was Rami.)

But she was waiting for him to come back.

And while she waited, she scratched the wall again.

A Girl, Once Upon a Time

Once upon a time, there was a girl.

Who was not stuck at a museum.

But who, instead, felt stuck on her family's apple orchard.

She loved her family, and she loved being outside, but she longed for . . . something else. She knew that it existed somewhere else in the world. She wanted to seek it out.

She turned to drawing as a way to imagine the something else.

Art, she understood, was a wish that you made with your hands.

One afternoon, when she was hiding out from her family, sitting under an apple tree, sketch pad balanced against her knees, a boy approached her.

"Hello," he said. "What are you drawing?"

She held up her sketchbook for him to see.

Before he said anything, she could see in his eyes that he saw it.

That something else.

She smiled. She knew they were going to be friends.

Cinnamon Rolls and a Surprise Day Off

"I have the day off," Rami's mother announced.

"What?" Rami said. He sat up in bed and rubbed his eyes.

Rami's mother opened the blinds. Pale and watery sunlight leaked into the room. Rami rubbed his eyes again.

He had been counting on going back to the Penelope today. He needed to talk to the floating girl. He needed to see if she was still there.

A big part of his brain was sure that he had imagined her. That she had never really been there at all.

"But," Rami said, "you always work on Tuesdays."

"Not today." His mother gave him a forced smile. "Which is great news, isn't it? This means we can spend the day together."

Rami frowned. "Did Dr. Hale ask you not to come in?"

His mother's forced smile stayed planted on her face. It managed to somehow be both brighter than a light bulb and as fake and fluorescent as one, too. "The detectives or police or whoever are coming today. Dr. Hale thought it would be best to call all of us in for questioning later, one by one."

Rami sat up further. He grabbed the stuffed-animal shark, aptly named Sharkie, that he still slept with. The story was his mother had bought it in the Atlanta airport when his parents had first arrived in America.

"Why are you smiling when talking about being investigated?"

"Because I'm not being investigated. I'm being questioned."

"Same difference."

"There's nothing to worry about," she said.

Rami begged to differ. There was a lot to worry about. Namely, the fact that the painting was missing. And it was really starting to seem like Dr. Hale and the other people at the museum thought his mom might have had something to do with it. Not to mention there was also a strange girl floating around the

Penelope who only he could see.

There was indeed a lot to worry about. Rami swallowed.

"And because I have the day off, we can go to the library. And the library is always a reason to smile."

His mom pinched his cheek, and he groaned.

"Mom," he said. "I'm almost twelve."

He realized this statement probably didn't have the oomph he wanted because he was hugging a stuffed shark.

"And that means you're too old for the library?"

"No. Never. Just that you should stop pinching my cheek." He touched his face. "Besides, it hurts."

"Oh." His mom leaned over and kissed the top of his head. "What do the kids say these days, 'sorry not sorry'? Go ahead and get dressed. We can get breakfast on our way."

Rami groaned. "That's not what that phrase means."

"Get ready!" his mom hollered over her shoulder as she glided out of the room. "I'm craving cinnamon scones from Benny's. What do you think?"

Now Rami knew something was truly wrong. Pizza last night, breakfast treats today. His mother never spent money like this. Or allowed him to eat so many meals in a row with neither a fruit nor a vegetable in sight.

Once Rami was dressed, he grabbed his backpack and carefully and secretively snatched the copy of yesterday's newspaper, slipping it into the front zippered pocket.

"Ready?" his mom asked as she shrugged on her coat and fished around for her keys. Her coat did not fit her. It was way too big. But she'd found it at the thrift store and fell in love with its bright blue jewel color.

"This is going to be great," she said as she locked the apartment door behind them. It felt more like a motivational speech she was giving herself than a true proclamation about the day, but Rami went along with it.

They walked side by side down the stairwell, the sound of their footsteps dulled by the carpeted steps. The stairwell had recently been recarpeted. The apartment complex had bragged about it. And then raised the rent. Again.

"Will you go back to work tomorrow?"

"Maybe."

"Mom."

"Rami, don't worry."

"When you say that, I only worry more."

She grabbed him by his shoulders and bopped her nose against his. She laughed, and he laughed a little, too, but still said, "Mom."

"I know, I know. You're almost twelve."

"Do you think they'll for sure call you in for questioning today?"

"Rami," his mom said. "Let it go. It's going to be okay."

Rami jumped off the last step. For a brief second, he enjoyed the sensation of flying.

His mom opened the door, and a cold breeze greeted them. Rami zipped his jacket up all the way to his neck. The sun was bright, but the air still had most of its winter sharpness.

On their journey to the library, they passed other Maple Lake residents who were out and about. Rami didn't know most of them. He saw one or two kids from his school. He waved half-heartedly because his mom waved enthusiastically.

He wondered if when those kids saw him, they thought about that one terrible day at school. The day he'd been humiliated in front of everyone. His throat felt tight, but he forced himself to wave.

Almost as if his mom could read his mind, she

said, "Hey, I haven't heard you talk about Matty or Henry in a while. How are they?"

Rami swallowed. "Um," he said. "They're good."

Or at least he assumed they were good without him. And that felt not so good.

"Do you think you'll see them over break? I'd be happy for them to come over to our place."

Rami looked at his shoes. "Um, yeah, sure, maybe."

Thankfully his mom didn't press it any further because she got distracted by a bird. Which was a very common occurrence for his mom.

"Look," his mom said, pointing at a tree.

It took Rami a second to spot the red-winged blackbird. He knew red-winged blackbirds were migratory birds. Seeing them was a sign of spring.

His mother had taught him that. She loved all animals. Especially birds. She read about them and researched them, and sometimes, on her days off, she would paint them. Or, more specifically, she would make paintings that when you looked at them a certain way, you were able to see a bird.

Rami called those paintings "surprise birds." Every time he found the hidden beak or the camouflaged wing, he would experience a surge of delightful satisfaction.

After walking for a while, they finally reached Benny's, the local bakery. He and his mom both ordered a cinnamon scone. Rami ate his in two quick giant bites. His mother ate hers in four.

"So good," his mom said.

"So good," Rami answered.

"We're going to be okay," his mom said, wiping a stray crumb from his mouth.

He almost moved his face away from his mother's touch, but he didn't. He leaned into her.

A Connection at the Library

Rami saw Veda before she saw him. She was browsing a display of books about dragons.

He debated saying hi, but he always found that initial approach so awkward. He never wanted to bother anyone. How do you know if someone actually wants you to say hi? Rami found that very hard to figure out.

So, he didn't say hi. He walked over to one of the computers and dutifully entered his library membership number, which he, of course, had memorized.

"Playing a game?" Veda said. She sat down next to him. She spun around in the computer chair, kicking out her legs.

"Oh," Rami said. "Hi."

"Hi yourself," Veda answered, click-clacking on the keyboard. Veda was wearing a bright orange sweater. Rami assumed it was one that her mom had knitted. Veda complained a lot about how her mom was constantly knitting things, but she always wore the sweaters. Rami liked that about Veda.

As of a few months ago, Rami ate lunch at the same table as Veda. Veda's lunch table had taken him in after everything bad went down with his old friends. He didn't really talk with anyone at the new table. He was scared that if he did, they might remember he was there and make him leave. So, he quietly ate his school-approved SunButter-and-jelly sandwich and listened. And Veda was a loud and frequent talker at lunch, which was how he knew all about Veda's mom's knitted sweaters.

"I like your sweater."

"Thanks. My mom made it." Veda craned her neck to look at Rami's screen. "Ooh, you're looking up the same thing I am."

"Yeah . . . uh . . ."

"Your mom works there, yeah?"

Rami nodded. He minimized his browser.

"You don't have to be shy, Rami Ahmed. And don't worry, I don't think your mom stole the painting." She tipped her head back. "I have my own theories."

"Really?"

"Yeah. I think some rich dudes stole it."

"Why would some rich dudes have stolen it?"

Veda shrugged. "Isn't it usually rich dudes that steal art?"

"I don't know about that." Rami clicked on the window he had minimized. A picture of the painting popped up. He looked right at the girl from the painting's green eyes. He shivered and broke eye contact with the screen.

"I don't think rich dudes have to steal paintings. I think they can just buy them," Rami said.

"It's probably fun or something for them to steal paintings. Like a sport. Like shooting elephants. Isn't it terrible that rich dudes shoot elephants?"

"Not sure if that's true."

"Oh, it definitely is. I've seen pictures of it."

Rami had also seen the sad elephant photos. "I meant the other thing. That rich dudes steal paintings for fun."

"Do you have a better theory?"

He thought about the girl floating in Cherry Hall. He shook his head.

Veda crossed her arms and spun around in her chair again. "That's what I thought."

"I just know it wasn't my mom."

"No one thinks it was your mom."

Rami made a snorting sound.

"Wait. Someone *really* thinks it's your mom?"

Veda knew Rami's mom a little bit because in second grade, Rami and Veda had been partners during the solar system project. Veda had come over to Rami's apartment, and they'd made a model of Jupiter out of Styrofoam. Rami's mom had let them use her acrylic paint to decorate it, and Veda had been really excited about that.

While they'd worked on the Jupiter project, Veda had asked him, "Where was your mom born?"

"Lebanon," Rami had said.

"Oh, cool, my parents are from India," Veda replied.

They didn't talk about it anymore—the fact that both of them had parents who had been born in different countries—but Rami felt like there was an understanding between them. It was possible this was just in his head, though. Lots of things these days seemed to only be in his head.

"Rami Ahmed, answer me," Veda insisted.

Rami fidgeted. He looked over his shoulder. His mom was still browsing the adult science-fiction aisle.

He knew she was looking for a book about robots. His mom loved robots. Almost as much as she loved birds.

"Where's your mom?" Rami asked.

"With Aditi."

Aditi was Veda's little sister.

"Doing what?"

"Stealing paintings."

Rami's eyes widened. "What?"

"I'm joking. They're obviously checking out books for Aditi."

"I don't know how obvious that is," Rami mumbled.

"Dude, it's pretty obvious. We're in a library. What do people do in a library?"

"Check out books."

"Ba-boom. There you go. Anyway, spill. Who thinks your mom stole the painting? The police?"

"I shouldn't be talking about this."

"I can help you, you know," Veda said.

Rami typed some other words into the search engine. H. F. Bottemtow, *Untitled*, girl in painting, name and age. The screen populated with a bunch of results. He clicked on the first one. "I don't think you can."

"I already know a lot of things. I'm like this close to cracking the case." Veda pinched her fingers together. "This close."

"And your main theory is that it's rich dudes?"

"No. That's just what I say to unserious people."

"You said it to me."

"I thought maybe you were unserious about the investigation."

Rami turned to face her. "You thought I was unserious about not wanting my mom to go to jail for a crime she didn't commit?"

"Whoa. I'm sorry." Veda held her hands up. "I didn't know your mom was in such big trouble."

"It was stolen during the deep clean."

Veda wrinkled her nose. "The deep clean?"

Rami sighed. "I thought you knew everything about the case."

"Like, I do. But . . ."

"My mom was working when the painting was stolen," Rami explained.

"Oh. Well, I knew that. Why didn't you just say that?"

"I kind of did."

"No, you didn't." Veda leaned back in the computer chair. Rami worried for a moment that she might tip over. "Anyway, you want to hear my theory? My *real* theory?"

Rami was about to say yes when he heard his mother's clomping boots behind him. This was one of the reasons he was absolutely sure she hadn't stolen the painting. She wasn't the slightest bit stealthy.

He quickly clicked out of everything on his screen.

"Rami, we need to go," his mom said.

He spun around to face her. "What? Why? We just got here."

Rami's mother saw Veda. "Oh, hi, Veda. It's nice to see you again. You've gotten so tall."

Rami groaned, but Veda beamed. "It's good to see you, too, Ms. Ahmed."

Rami's mother touched his arm. "Come on. Let's go."

"Are you going to the Penelope?" Veda asked.

"Veda," Rami said through clenched teeth.

Rami's mother gave Veda one of her forced smiles. "As a matter of fact, we are. But I'm sure we'll be back at the library again sometime soon. Hopefully we will run into you some other time. I know Rami would like that."

"Mom," Rami groaned again. His face burned.

Veda sprang out of her chair. "Can I come with you?"

"Um." Rami's mother looked around the library. Probably searching for Veda's mom. "Would that be okay with your parents?"

"Definitely," Veda said. "Let me just check really quick."

While Veda ran off to find her mom, Rami said, "I didn't tell her anything. I swear."

Rami's mom ruffled his hair.

"Mom," Rami said again, pushing her hand away.

"I know you didn't say anything, habibi. It might be nice for you to bring a friend to the museum, though. We could be there awhile."

Rami searched her face for any clues about what was going on. "Is it Dr. Hale who called? Is it your turn to be questioned?"

His mother nodded. She had a faraway look in her eyes. Rami pretended she was thinking about robots. Or birds. Even though he knew she probably wasn't.

"Good news!" Veda called out as she dashed back toward the computers. "I can come with you!"

"Great," Rami's mother said. "And you're sure it's okay with your mom?"

"Yeah, I told her she could pick me up at your place later."

Rami gaped at Veda. "You're coming over to our house?"

It had been a really long time since he'd had a friend over.

"Yeah. That's not a problem, is it?"

Rami's mother smiled. And it wasn't a forced one. "Not a problem at all."

In Which the Floating Girl Is Given a Name

The museum was crowded when they arrived for Rami's mother's questioning. She disappeared into the upstairs room, where no one from the public was supposed to go. She left Rami and Veda downstairs, sitting beside Ed, who was supposed to keep an eye on them.

And of course it had to be Ed who was working instead of Theodore. Even though Rami was never quite sure how to talk with Theodore, he was still much better than Ed. Because Ed was, well, Ed.

"Are we allowed to look at the art?" Veda asked.

Ed leaned forward on his elbows. He was sitting on a wooden stool behind a big desk near the front entrance. "Are you going to steal anything?"

Rami did what he had good practice doing during

lunch at school—he feigned polite laughter.

"It's not funny," Ed said.

"Oh," Rami said. "I thought you were making a joke."

One large vein in Ed's forehead noticeably twitched. "Do you think the fact the painting is missing is a joke?"

"No," Rami said quickly. "We just want to look at the other art. The art that is still here."

"Haven't you seen it already?"

Rami shrugged. Clearly, he wanted to look for the floating girl. But (also clearly) it wasn't like he could say that to Ed. "Doesn't Dr. Hale say you can always find something new at the Penelope?"

"Yeah," Veda added. "She does say that."

Rami was pretty sure Veda had never heard Dr. Hale say that. That she had never talked to Dr. Hale before in her life.

Veda tapped her foot in a way that projected confidence. "And plus, it's not like *I've* seen everything."

Ed puckered his lips. "Fine. You two can walk around. But I'll be watching you." He pointed to the security camera footage that was streaming in front of him. "At all times," he added.

"Looks like the cameras are working again," Rami said.

"They most certainly are. Theodore and I have made sure of that. No more funny business."

Rami gave him a salute. Ed frowned. Maybe that had been the wrong move. Rami considered apologizing but ultimately decided that saying nothing was better. He scurried off with Veda into the public part of the museum.

"Have you ever seen someone?" Rami said, and then realized how profoundly weird it sounded.

"What?"

"Never mind."

"No. You asked me if I'd ever seen someone. I think I'm seeing you right now, yeah?"

"Yeah." Rami stopped walking. They were in Plum Hall. All the halls were named after fruits. This was because Penelope L. Brooks, the person whom the museum was named for, had loved fruits. This information was listed on a small silver plaque at the entrance to the museum. Most people didn't read it.

Rami had read it at least a hundred times.

He shared this fact with Veda.

"Huh?" Veda said. She shook her head. "Rich

people are weird. I would not have named the rooms after fruits."

"What would you have named them after?"

"Jungle cats. Obviously."

Rami smiled. "Obviously."

"Come on. Jaguar Hall sounds epic. No one would try to steal a painting from Jaguar Hall."

At the mention of a stolen painting, Rami instinctively looked over his shoulder. He didn't want anyone to overhear him them talking about the theft. The Penelope was full of visitors today. Ever since *Untitled* had gone missing, ticket sales were up. Way, way up.

"You said you had a theory," Rami said in a low voice.

"Oh. Yeah," Veda said in a voice that could in no way be described as low.

"We probably shouldn't talk about . . . you know . . . very loudly."

"What is 'you know'?"

"You know."

"No. I don't. If I did, I wouldn't be asking."

"The theft," Rami whispered.

"Oh. My bad. That should've been obvious to me since you did ask me about my theory, yeah?"

"Yeah," Rami said as nicely as he could.

"I think it was someone at the museum."

"Veda!" Rami said. This time his tone was a little more pointed.

"What?"

"That's not helpful. That's why people think it's my mom."

Visitors threaded around them, the herringbone wooden floors of the Penelope creaking under their feet. Veda and Rami shifted through the crowd—families with kids who seemed like they wanted to be anywhere other than here and families with kids who were bursting with excitement, old couples and young couples, and people who had the harried but also satisfied look of someone who'd traveled a long distance to be here.

"Oh, sorry. Well, I don't think it was your mom. But maybe someone else who works at the museum?"

Rami let that thought roll around in his brain. As much as he disliked Ed, he couldn't think of a single person from the museum who he really believed would've stolen the painting.

Rami and Veda turned the corner. They were both instinctively walking toward Cherry Hall. As they made their way in that direction, the crowd grew thicker.

"Everyone wants to see it," Veda said.

"But they can't. It's gone."

Before it was a museum, the Penelope had been a house that had belonged to the wealthy Brooks family, titans of the railroad industry. Much of the interior of the Victorian mansion had been gutted when it had been turned into a museum, so it was easy to forget that it had ever been a house. The wooden framed archway that marked the entrance to Cherry Hall was one of the few reminders.

Pushing past a man who was chewing gum, Rami stepped into Cherry Hall. The air smelled like cinnamon. You weren't supposed to chew gum in the museum. But it was Ed's job to monitor that.

Rami scanned the room. He'd never seen so many people in Cherry Hall. None of the faces here were the one he was looking for, though.

"It used to be right there, yeah?" Veda pointed at the blank white space that many people were gathered around.

Rami nodded. The marks were still there. He was about to point them out to Veda when a voice said, "You've returned."

Rami turned. It was the girl. The floating girl.

"Veda," Rami said. "Do you see her?"

Veda moved closer to him. Around them, bodies shuffled. Everyone jostling for a chance to look at the empty wall.

"Yes. I'm here. Sadly, I have not managed to go anywhere else," the girl said.

"Are you talking about her?" Veda said.

"You see her, too?" Rami asked.

The girl put her hands on her hips. Rami tried his best not to stare at her feet.

"You know, it is rather rude to talk about people right in front of them," the girl said. "You should save that for when I'm not here. Though the miserable fact of the matter is that I'm always here."

"Uh, whoa," Veda said. "Why aren't you wearing shoes? And, oh, yikes, what is going on with your feet?"

The girl looked down at her feet. Rami did, too. He couldn't help it. The girl shrugged. "This is simply how I am. I float. I recognize that's quite unusual, but I have no explanation for it. As for my lack of shoes, that is another mystery. Currently, I appear to contain a multitude of mysteries."

Veda squished up her face. Her mouth hung open.

"I know," Rami said. "Weird, right?"

"Don't be rude, Rami," Veda whispered at him. Then she added, "Does anyone else see her?"

The girl shook her head. "I can answer that."

"Well," Veda said, frowning at the girl. "What's the answer, then?"

The girl shook her head some more. "I am fairly confident the answer is no."

"Why can we see you?" Veda asked.

"For that, I do not have a good explanation." The girl shrugged again. To watch someone shrug while floating was quite an odd sight. Rami felt like letting out a tiny scream. But he swallowed it down.

"Perhaps we are connected," the girl said.

"How would we be connected?" Veda asked.

"Another mystery," the girl said.

"Have you seen her before?" Veda kept switching her attention between Rami and the girl.

"Yes. Once," Rami said.

"I have, like, so many questions," said Veda.

"As do I," the girl said.

Rami had lots of questions, too. But he was sure Veda would tell him that was obvious. So, he kept his mouth shut.

People continued to stream in and out of Cherry

Hall. Rami listened to fragments of conversations.

"*There it is*," people would say.

"*That's where the painting used to hang.*"

"*What's the name of the painting that was stolen again?*"

"*What? That's so strange. Why doesn't it have a name?*"

From overhearing conversations, Rami felt confident that no one was aware that he and Veda were talking with anyone else, let alone a floating ghost girl. They were too obsessed with the blank white space to pay attention to what was happening right in front of them.

Veda's mouth was stuck in a wide-open O of surprise and shock. She kept staring at the girl. Mostly at her feet. Which Rami found quite relatable.

"This is wild," Veda said. "Who are you? And why do you float? And why—"

"I truly do not know," the girl said. "I can't quite make sense of any of this."

"Don't you recognize her?" Rami asked.

"Her?" the girl and Veda said at the same time.

"I'm sorry, but I do not think we have ever met. But given my current state, I cannot say that with any sort of true confidence. Considering I don't even know my own name," the girl said.

"My name is Veda," Veda said slowly.

"Very pleased to meet you, Veda."

"Nice to meet you, too." Veda pointed at Rami. "And that's Rami. I don't know if he introduced himself to you yet or not."

The girl smiled. "He most certainly did not."

"I was going to," Rami mumbled. He nudged Veda. "Look at her."

"I am looking at her." Veda waved at the girl. "Hello."

"Hello," said the girl.

"Don't you see?" Rami asked.

"See what?" Veda and the girl both said.

"Uh, it's really confusing when you two talk at the same time," Rami said, and then continued, "She's the girl from the painting."

Veda studied the floating girl. She squinted at her. "Holy moly," she finally said.

"I'm the what?" the floating girl asked.

"You're the girl from the painting," Veda said. "Rami's right. The girl who's standing under the apple tree."

"I do not have the faintest clue what you mean by that," the girl said. "I do not see any apple trees in this room."

Rami wished he had his backpack with him. If he had, he would've pulled out the newspaper article and showed the floating girl. But Ed had made him leave his backpack behind the big desk at the front entrance.

"You know about the painting that went missing, right?" Veda said.

"Of course. It is the only subject anyone around here ever discusses. I am already quite bored of hearing about it, to be honest. It was interesting at first, but—"

"It's you," Veda interrupted. "Or at least someone who looks exactly like you. In the painting, I mean. You are in the painting. The painting that's missing."

"Hmm." The girl considered this. "That might make sense."

"How could that possibly make sense?" The loudness of Rami's own voice surprised him. "I think . . ."

Worried that he was drawing attention to their little group, he scanned the room again.

Most of the crowd was still jostling for a place in line to stare at the blank white wall. Rami waited to overhear a comment about the scratches. But he didn't hear one. He only heard people's theories.

"It was definitely an inside job."

"Had to be."

"Who else could turn off the cameras?"

"Earth to Rami," Veda said.

He blinked. "Oh, sorry."

"You were saying something. It sounded like you had some kind of epiphany."

"Epiphany," Rami said. He looked at the floating girl. "Maybe that's what we should call you. For now. Until we figure out your real name."

"Naw," Veda said, and then turned to face the girl. "You're not that serious and stuffy, are you?"

Rami considered the way the girl spoke. Her formal and lilting tone. He kind of disagreed with Veda's assessment, but he kept his mouth shut.

"I don't know what I am." She stared down at her floating feet. "I wish that I had even the slightest idea."

The girl sounded very sad. Rami briefly thought about the lunch table that he was no longer welcome at. He wanted to say something encouraging, but he wasn't sure what.

"How about Blue?" Veda said. "Because of your blue dress."

The girl pinched her lips together, puzzling over the suggestion. "I suppose that's fine. It is a name. A name feels like a start."

Rami still liked Epiphany better. But Blue worked, too.

"It's a name," Veda said, and then she added, "Until we figure out your real one."

In Which Our Turtle Decides to Become an Artist

Agatha noticed the woman before the woman noticed her.

Turtles most often see things before humans do.

Agatha noticed many things about the woman. She noticed that the woman came to the garden behind the Penelope at almost the exact same time every day. That the woman smelled like chemicals and artificial pine but underneath that antiseptic stench was the lovely smell of rose water.

She also noticed that the woman was sadly a very neat eater. Which meant that there were never any crumbs left over from her lunch. Which looked delicious—cucumbers and feta cheese and pita bread.

But most of all, she noticed that after the woman was done eating, she would draw.

She always drew for ten minutes. Never more. Never less.

It was difficult from Agatha's vantage point to always see what the woman was drawing. Agatha tried different positions. Sometimes she could crane to get a small glimpse. But mostly, she just had to imagine.

Then, one day, after the woman finished drawing, she turned in Agatha's direction. She held out her sketchbook. She showed it to her.

"It's you, Agatha," the woman said. "How about that for a name?"

"What do you think?" the woman asked.

Agatha, of course, could not answer.

But she looked at the drawing. The drawing of her.

And as she looked, she was filled with an indescribable feeling. The feeling of being seen.

She wanted to capture that feeling. She wanted to give it to another being.

She wanted to draw.

16

The Creation of *Untitled*

The girl who had once sketched under the apple trees in her parents' orchard grew up to be a young woman who sketched under the apple trees in her parents' orchard.

But now it was time for her to leave the apple orchard. To go in search of that something else that she was seeking.

Before she left, she gave a painting to the boy whom she had shown a sketch to once upon a time. It was the first painting she had ever fully finished.

The boy whom she had once shown a sketch to was now a young man.

She knew that he would understand the painting. That he would see what she was trying to show him.

"What's the name of the painting?" he asked.

"It doesn't have one."

He smiled slightly. "*Untitled* for now. I get it."

"I knew you would," she said.

It is a singular feeling to be understood. Seen. Connected.

It is the best feeling in the whole world.

A Plan Begins to Form

"Why do you think no one else can see Blue?" Veda asked Rami. She was sprawled out on his bedroom floor with a copy of the *Maple Lake Ledger.*

She was staring at the reprinted picture of *Untitled.* Rami knew she was checking her own brain, comparing what she saw in the painting with what she remembered about Blue.

He knew because he had done the exact same thing after seeing Blue for the first time.

Rami sat on the ground next to his bed. "I have no idea."

"I think you're right, though. Blue probably appeared in the museum right after *Untitled* was taken. Her being there has something to do with the theft," Veda said. "My dad says that there is a pattern to everything. You just have to look for it. So what's the pattern here? What are we missing? Maybe she knew H. F. Bottemtow? Do you think that's it?"

The word "dad" rolled effortlessly off Veda's tongue. He thought of the mustached man from the Photo. He wondered what it would be like to say that word so easily.

One of Rami's mother's surprise-bird paintings was hanging on the wall. He looked at it. For a moment, he couldn't find the bird. But after blinking a few times, he was able to find the wings again.

Veda propped up her elbows. "Can we just say it?"

"Say wh—"

Veda interrupted him. "She's a ghost. She's a ghost, right?"

A chill rolled through Rami. He rubbed his arms. "I don't know."

"She has to be a ghost." Veda held up a finger. "Not everyone can see her." She held up another finger. "And two, she floats." She put up one more finger. "And lastly, she's kind of spooky."

"I don't know if she's spooky." He thought about her floating feet. "I guess she's a little spooky."

"She's a ghost," Veda said again.

"Well, that means she's dead," Rami said slowly. The words, particularly that last one, tasted wrong in

Rami's mouth. He didn't know Blue that well. But he didn't like to think about her being . . . dead.

"Jeez. That's a little harsh, yeah?"

"I mean, isn't being dead a requirement for being a ghost?"

Veda tilted her head, considering this. "I guess you're right."

"Yeah. I think I am."

Veda looked back at the photo of *Untitled*. "We need to figure out who H. F. Bottemtow was painting. That's who Blue is, probably?"

"Yeah."

"So, we're looking for a dead person that H. F. Bottemtow painted a long time ago?"

"Yeah," Rami said again.

"And no one knows who this girl is?"

"Yeah," Rami said once more.

Veda held up the newspaper. "These articles don't tell us enough about H. F. Bottemtow."

Rami sighed. "No one knows a lot about her."

"She's not dead, though. So Blue can't be her, right? At least we've ruled out one person. Only seven point eight billion more to go." Veda pointed at the newspaper. "It says here that she's living at Evergreen Pines. We should go visit her."

Rami shook his head. "Lots of people have already tried that. Evergreen Pines isn't letting anyone in. H. F. Bottemtow doesn't want to talk to anyone."

Veda raised her eyebrows. "Maybe that's because she stole the painting?"

"I doubt it. Why would she steal her own painting?"

Veda pulled herself into a sitting position. "I don't know. It's probably weird to make something and then not have it belong to you anymore. I could see wanting it back. Think about it."

Rami did think about it. He thought making something seemed terrifying. To put yourself out there like that. He guessed he could imagine wanting whatever he had made back, but he could barely imagine giving it away in the first place.

"We should go to Evergreen Pines," Veda said.

"But they're not—"

"Yeah, yeah. I know they're not letting anyone in. But we should sneak in."

"How?"

Veda smiled. "I'm sure we can come up with something."

Lies and More Lies

Rami was not skilled at lying. Then again, he'd never had much reason to lie.

"I'm going to see Veda," he told his mom.

That wasn't a lie. But it still made his insides feel like a sponge that was being squeezed. Ever since sixth grade had started, he'd begun to keep more and more things from his mom. But this one felt pretty big.

His mom didn't seem to notice anything was off, though. She was rushing around, getting ready for work. Two of the people who used to be on her crew had quit because of the hoopla with the missing painting. His mom was clearly upset about this development.

"It makes it seem like something fishy happened," she said. "Which it didn't."

"I know it didn't," Rami said. "Hey, I'm going to see Veda," he tried again. The insides-squeezing feeling grew.

"Veda?" his mom said, bending down to kiss him on the forehead. "That's great, habibi. That's nice that you guys are hanging out more. Her mom will be there, right?"

Rami's throat was dry. He nodded. He didn't trust his voice.

"Will anyone else be there? Like maybe Matty? I haven't seen him in a while."

Rami shook his head.

His mom gave him a look. He worried she was going to ask some more questions. But instead, she said, "I can drop you at her house before I go to the Penelope."

Rami's insides squeezed again. "Uh," he coughed. "We're meeting at the library?" He meant it as a statement. But it came out like a question.

His mom slipped on her oversized blue-jewel-colored coat. "Great. Let's go to the library."

Rami held his breath the whole walk to the library. Okay, that's not exactly true. Because it would be physically impossible. But he *felt* like he was holding his breath the whole way.

"Hey, Rami," Veda said. She was standing in front of the library just like she said she would be. She was wearing her backpack and a yellow knitted hat.

"Hi, Veda," Rami's mother said. "I love your hat. Did your mama make it?"

Veda beamed. "Yes, she did."

Rami's mother admired the fur bob on the top of the hat. "I love it!"

"Thank you."

"Do you know where she learned to knit like that?" Rami's mother inspected the hat some more. "She has great craftmanship."

"She picked it up when she first moved here from India. She was really lonely when she first came, and she said it started as a way to make friends, but now she loves it because she always wants to be doing something with her hands." Veda fluttered her own hands in the air to demonstrate this point.

Rami's mom smiled. "That makes so much sense. I know what that's like. It can be hard when you first arrive here, and a little lonely. . . ."

His mom trailed off. Rami searched her face. He thought of how she looked in the photo he had found, the way her arms wrapped around the mustached man's neck. Had she been lonely then, too, or did that only come after?

His mom shook her head, as if tossing aside a daydream. "Anyway, speaking of your mama, is she here? Can I talk with her real quick? I just want to check with her about when I should pick up Rami."

Veda shuffled her feet. It was barely detectable, but Rami noticed. He held his breath again.

"She's helping Aditi in the bathroom right now. But she said we could just call you when Rami was ready to be picked up. Does that work?" Veda stretched her smile to be even wider than before.

Rami knew that response wasn't going to work. This was his mom who dragged him with her to work. Who never let him stay alone in their apartment. Who worried all the time about his safety. There was no possible way—

"That sounds perfect." Rami's mom gave him a tight hug. "Have fun. I'll wait for your call after work."

Once his mom was a safe distance from the library, Rami let out the biggest exhale of his life.

"No way that just happened," he said.

Veda was still smiling. "It happened." She glanced down at her watch. It had a bright purple plastic wristband patterned with yellow stars. "Bus leaves in ten minutes. We need to hurry."

She took off running, and Rami followed her.

"I can't believe it," he said again, jogging beside her. He was, of course, thrilled. But there was also a nagging hunch that something was up with his mom. Something was different. And it wasn't good.

He tried not to think about it for too long.

"That was the easy part. Now the adventure begins," Veda said.

At that moment, the bus pulled up at the curb. Its doors opened with a squealing whine. Veda confidently bounded up the steps. She pulled a card out of her pocket and swiped it. "He's with me," she said to the bus driver, and swiped again for Rami.

Rami blinked at the driver, who waved him through. He fought the urge to tiptoe as he walked behind Veda. He was sure that at any second someone was going to jump up and grab him, catch him—well, he wasn't sure what they would catch him doing. Being here? Lying to his mom about where he was spending the day?

He took a deep breath. The bus smelled like stale french fries. Which inexplicably made Rami kind of hungry. But then he remembered his mom had no idea he was on this bus, and the craving for french fries went away.

"You need to chill out," Veda said once they'd found two seats next to one another. "You're practically shaking. Take a deep breath."

Rami looked around. No one was looking back. "Where does your mom think you are?"

"With you."

"No, I mean—"

"At your house," Veda further explained.

Rami could feel himself sweating. He took a few more deep breaths. "And my mom thinks I'm—"

"At my house. Just like we planned. Try not to stress so much. Chill out, my friend." Veda grinned triumphantly. She pulled a stack of papers out of her backpack. And then fished out a bright orange highlighter.

At the words "my friend," Rami found himself smiling. And chilling out. Not a lot. But it was a start.

"What's that?" he asked, eyeing what she'd pulled out of her backpack.

"Research. You'll never believe what I found last night."

Outside the bus windows, streets passed by. They were moving farther and farther away from their part of Maple Lake. Heading away from the museum and the library and the bakery and the lake the town was named for and heading toward the cornfields and the apple orchards and the endless sprawl of open land.

And Evergreen Pines.

As Rami looked out the window, he saw a lone goose at the edge of a field. All the other geese were gathered on the opposite side. He watched the lone goose wander around by itself. He blinked, and for a moment Rami was struck with the sensation that he wasn't moving. Only the world around him was.

Veda tapped his shoulder. "Did you hear me?" She followed his gaze out the window. "Wait. What do you see?"

He swallowed. He wasn't sure if he should share. But he took a deep breath and decided to. "Nothing. Just the world. It's like it's moving, and I'm . . . I don't know. I'm not?"

Veda screwed up her face, making a baffled expression. Rami's face felt hot. He wished he could grab back the words that he'd said. This was the type of thing that had gotten him in trouble with Henry and Matty. They'd told him he was weird.

He bit his tongue.

But then Veda's face relaxed, and she smiled

softly. "Yeah. I sometimes get that feeling, too."

The heat in his face stayed, but he smiled. "You do?"

"Yeah, I do. But hey," Veda said. She scooted closer to him. "I was saying that I found some good stuff last night. I printed off every article I could find about the Penelope. Because I was trying to see if we could come up with some names we don't know."

Rami turned from the window to Veda. "Names we don't know?"

"Yeah. Of people who used to work at the Penelope. So we could come up with some suspects. Remember my main theory?"

He shrugged. Veda was full of theories. He wasn't quite sure which one was the main one. "That Blue is a ghost?"

Veda kicked her feet out in front of her. "No. That's a theory, yes. But not the main one."

See? It was hard to keep track of all of them.

"The main one is that the person who stole the painting works or used to work at the museum." Before Rami could interject, Veda lightly touched his shoulder. "And I know what you're going to say. So, I'll state again, on the record, I obviously don't think your mom did it. Though we can't fully rule her out.

Because that would be sloppy detective work."

Rami had a billion questions. But he was finding that's how it usually went with Veda. Talking with Veda sometimes felt like drinking straight out of a hose—it all came at you very fast, at full blast.

But he was finding it was pretty nice to be in the splash zone.

"And before you ask," Veda continued, "I know a lot about detective work from listening to *Once Upon a Chilly Night*." Again, she dug in her backpack. This time she pulled out a tablet. Rami was a little bit jealous. He did not have a device of his own.

"Have you ever listened to this podcast? It's narrated by Alex Vincenzo. She used to work as a detective and now does deep dives into all these unsolved cases from years ago. I've just learned a bunch of things from Alex. It also helps me to fall asleep at night. I know that might sound strange, but there's something comforting about knowing someone is out there solving crimes. But never mind about Alex—we need to figure out who works at the museum. And who used to work at the museum. And who would have a motive."

She shoved the tablet back into her bag. Rami resisted the urge to ask if she had any games downloaded. It didn't seem like the right time.

"Wait. Am I talking too much?"

"What?" Rami said. "No. You're not—"

"Because my parents and other people sometimes tell me that I talk too much. I know I can be what adults call 'a lot.'"

Rami wasn't quite sure what to say. But he wanted to let her know that he understood. That he knew what it felt like to always feel wrong somehow. Like a right shoe placed on a left foot.

"You talk—"

"I know," she said quickly.

"I was trying to say . . . Well, I wanted to say . . . that you talk the right amount." He held his breath.

Veda smiled. "Really?"

"Really," Rami said.

"Cool," Veda said.

A few seconds later, she added, "Like, obviously. Right?"

"Yeah," Rami said, smiling a little. "Obviously."

The bus grinded to a stop. A few people stood to get off.

"Not our stop yet," Veda confirmed. "By the way, right now, my top suspect is Dr. Hale."

An alarm bell went off in Rami's brain. "Wait.

What?" He squinted at her, pulling his eyebrows together. "Dr. Hale wouldn't steal from her own museum."

"Or would she?" Veda tapped her highlighter against one of the many papers she was balancing on her lap. "It says here she was hired to increase attendance. And you and I both know that no one was going to the Penelope until the painting went missing."

"Some people were going," Rami mumbled.

Veda's lips twitched sympathetically. "You know what I mean. Did you see how crowded it was when we were there the other day?"

"Yeah, but I don't think Dr. Hale would do that. She cares about the museum too much."

Veda shook her head. "She has a motive, Rami. That's a big deal. People don't just commit crimes for no reason. Alex Vincenzo taught me that. Find the motive, you find your culprit."

"I'm sure there are other people with motives. What about someone who wanted to sell the painting for money?"

"Yeah. That's a good theory. But who at the museum needs money that badly?"

His mom's face popped into his mind. Nope. No

way. "I don't know," he said.

"Let's read through these. See if any names come up for you." Veda handed him a stack of papers.

They read for a while. Side by side. Rami would occasionally glance over. He wondered if Veda suspected his mom. He didn't think so. Plus, it's not like his mom necessarily needed money more than anyone else. They didn't have a lot of money. But they were fine. Weren't they?

He ran through the names of all the people he already knew. Mary Louise and Tony—both of whom had quit the cleaning crew yesterday. Terry and Shelly, who still worked on the cleaning crew. Ed and Theodore. Dr. Hale and her assistant, Maribeth.

Then he moved on to scan for names he didn't know. People who had once worked at the museum but didn't work there anymore. Most of the names washed over him. A name doesn't mean much when you can't place a face or a personality with it.

But then he stopped.

There was a name he recognized. Francesca Harding.

"Veda," Rami whispered.

Veda didn't answer. She was bent over, meticulously combing through all the articles she had printed.

"Veda," Rami said, this time a bit louder.

"What?"

"I found something. A name. I don't know if means anything, but look, Mrs. Harding used to work at the Penelope. Did you know that?"

Mrs. Harding had been their third-grade teacher. Rami had really liked her. She read aloud to them after recess, and she'd decorated her classroom with posters of great horned owls.

"Hmm." Veda craned her neck so she could see what Rami was pointing to. "I guess that's interesting. But you don't have any reason to think she stole the painting, do you?"

Rami deflated a bit. He'd been so excited to recognize a name that he had forgotten for a brief second what he was searching for. "No, but isn't it a little weird that Mrs. Harding never mentioned she worked at the Penelope? The whole time we were in her class?"

He pictured Mrs. Harding's face. Her short dark hair and animal-patterned socks. She didn't seem like an art thief, but did art thieves seem like art thieves?

"That is a little strange," Veda admitted. "But I still think Dr. Hale's motive is stronger."

"What about Ed?" Rami asked.

"Who's Ed?"

"The security guy. Or what about Theodore?"

Veda wrinkled her nose. "Why are you so obsessed with the security guys?"

Rami shifted in his seat. "I don't know. I guess they seem like the type that would understand how to steal a painting?"

"Motive, Rami." Veda tapped her highlighter again. "Remember, motive."

Ed seemed like the type of person who could have a motive. Maybe Theodore, too. Rami just needed to figure out what it would be.

Our Turtle Is a Dreamer

Humans might think that turtles don't dream, but they are wrong.

Or at least they were wrong about Agatha.

Agatha was a turtle who was full of dreams.

She wasn't sure if she'd always had dreams or if she'd learned to have them from spending so much time around the Penelope.

But what she knew for sure was that her interest in art had been kindled by that one special and specific interaction she'd had in the garden of the Penelope.

When Agatha awoke today, it was from a dream. A dream about art.

In this dream, she had been drawing a picture of the person she saw leave the museum with the painting. While she was drawing, she realized something.

She'd seen this person before.

At the museum.

It had taken her a moment to remember. But now she knew. She'd worked it out in her dream.

She knew exactly who had stolen the painting.

Disguises and Invisibility

Evergreen Pines was four blocks from the bus station. To her credit, Veda had mapped it out exactly.

But before they started the four-block walk, Veda handed Rami a hat from her bag. It was teal with a sparkly pom-pom on top.

"What am I supposed to do with this?"

"Wear it. Obviously."

"Thanks, but I'm okay. I don't need a hat. It's not even that cold out."

As if on cue, the wind blew, making Rami's ears cold. He gritted his teeth and refused to shiver.

Veda shook her head, laughing. "It's not to keep you warm. It's to disguise you. Remember the plan?"

Rami turned the hat over in his hands. The yarn was soft. He thought about his cold ears. "I don't think this is a disguise."

"Have you ever worn a sparkly teal hat before?"

"No."

"Exactly. Put it on."

Rami reluctantly tugged it on. The yarn felt even softer on his head. And very good on his cold ears. Wow. He wasn't exactly thrilled to be wearing a sparkly hat, but if he was being honest, he wasn't in any hurry to take it off, either.

As they walked to Evergreen Pines, Rami said, "I still don't think this qualifies as a disguise. Besides, you wear the hat you have on all the time."

"I do not."

"Well, I've seen you wear it before."

Veda stopped in her tracks. She took off her backpack and unzipped it. After replacing her yellow hat with a magenta one, she smiled at him.

"You have lots of hats," he said.

She nodded. "Lots and lots and lots of them."

"I still don't think these hats work as a disguise. It feels good on my head, though."

"Of course it does. My mom only uses the best yarn."

"Hey, Veda?"

"Yeah?"

"You said that people say you talk too much." Rami swallowed, but he pushed through. "Why do you think . . . ?"

"Ah," Veda said. "Well, when my friends say it, I think they're saying they're annoyed with me. And when my family says it, I guess it's another way of them telling me that I care about all the wrong things. Like my mom and dad just want me to get good grades and yada yada yada."

"What's yada yada yada?"

She grinned. "You know, college, becoming a doctor, yada yada yada."

"I know what that's like."

"Your mom wants you to be a doctor, too?"

Rami shook his head. "Just I know what it's like to not to be the person . . . other people seem to want you to be."

"You mean your old friends?"

Rami bit his tongue. He could feel something icy and jagged coiling inside him, a hesitation. Fear. He hadn't talked about this with anyone.

Veda continued to talk. "Don't worry about them. And I won't worry about the yada yada yada. Or I'll try not to. I'm going to be a detective, anyway. A *famous* detective."

There was so much Rami wanted to say, but all he could manage was "Okay."

Veda smiled, though. Which made him feel understood.

Soon, they found themselves in front of Evergreen Pines. It wasn't just one building, but many. There were standalone smaller buildings that looked like condos. There was an algae-covered pond. And there were even tennis courts. All the buildings were a shade of white that probably once was optimistically described as cream, and now would be more accurately described as white with dirt.

"Uh," Veda said. "I thought the tough part was going to be getting in. I didn't realize it was going to be figuring out where to go."

In the distance, Rami spotted a building that looked larger than all the rest. "Let's try there."

"What should we say when we walk in?" Veda asked.

"That we're here to see H. F. Bottemtow?"

Veda gaped at him. It was the same expression she'd made when she'd first seen Blue. And Blue's floating feet.

"I'm kidding," Rami said, smiling a little. It had been a while since he'd attempted any kind of joke.

“Oh. Right. I knew that. But really, what should we do?”

“I’m not sure. Maybe they won’t even notice us when we walk in?”

“Rami,” Veda said. “They’re definitely going to notice us.”

He thought about how he sat every day at Veda’s lunch table. How he stayed completely silent. How no one bothered to talk to him. But how that invisibility was better than being made fun of.

“Most people don’t notice me,” he said, and then immediately stared at the ground. He couldn’t believe he’d said that. Out loud.

“Dude, people notice you,” Veda said.

The icy feeling from before grew inside him, and he couldn’t help but remember that one terrible day at lunch. Even though he didn’t want to. The day Henry and Matty had humiliated him in front of everyone.

He saw himself walking up to their usual table holding his lunch tray. He saw Henry and Matty shaking their heads, refusing to let him sit down. He thought they were only joking at first. He’d tried to laugh. Remembering that part hurt the most.

His hands had trembled, and he’d backed up, accidentally bumping into another table. He lost control of his tray, chocolate milk sloshing onto his jeans. The sticky cold liquid dripping down into his socks. The tray had clattered as it hit the ground, echoing through the whole cafeteria. The silence of everyone's eyes on him, then the howling laughter.

"Rami." Veda waved her hand in front of his face, bringing him back. "It's true. Come on, now."

Rami shrugged. He kept looking at the ground.

"No, really," Veda said. "People notice you. And I don't mean that in a bad way. But in a good way."

Rami mustered the courage to look her in the eye. "Really?"

"Yeah. And this has given me an idea."

"What's that?"

She smiled. "Being invisible."

"Are you joking?"

She smiled wider. "No. I'm serious. Let's try it."

Unexpected Visitors

Unfortunately, the moment they stepped inside the building, they were most definitely noticed. So much for invisibility. A woman behind a desk greeted them.

"Nice hats," the woman said. "I really like those colors. Did your grandmother make them for you?"

"My mother," Veda answered.

"Oh," the woman said. "How nice. And now, who are you here to see?"

"Susan," Veda said, and Rami held his breath. He didn't know what Veda was doing.

"Susan Abraham, Susan Boyd, or Susan Gidwidtz?"

"Susan Boyd," Veda said.

"You know what room she's in?"

"I'm not sure. Can you tell me?" Veda said, smiling sweetly.

The lady looked up at Veda. Her eyes narrowed. "Wait a minute. How do you two know Susan?"

"We don't," Veda said. Her sweet smile widened. It was so sugary it almost gave Rami a toothache. "We're here to volunteer. Our school sent us. They said it's important to spend time with the elderly. We're here to read Ms. Susan Boyd a story."

Veda unzipped her backpack. She pulled out her tablet. "We were told Ms. Susan Boyd likes mysteries. And we have lots of mystery stories downloaded, ready to be read aloud."

"Oh my," the woman behind the desk said. "What darling and sweet kids you are. You'll find Susan in room 23. You just go down this hallway and turn right, and then left, and then right again. You got that?"

"Got it," Veda said.

Rami tried to smile at the lady. But he knew his smile did not look very sweet. Only nervous.

Once they were down the hall, Rami whispered, "How did you know to say we were here for Susan?"

"Lots of old ladies are named Susan."

Rami considered this.

"See? I'm like Detective Alex Vincenzo. I can think on my feet," Veda said.

"Are we really going to read to Susan?" Rami asked.

"Of course not! Besides, I never read off of my tablet. My tablet is for podcasts. I prefer to read actual books. Don't you? I like how they feel in my hands."

"Right," Rami said. "Okay, that's all great, but what are we going to do now? If we aren't going to read to Susan—"

"We're going to find H. F. Bottemtow's room!" Veda said, and then added, "Obviously."

Veda kept walking down the hall. Rami followed her. Veda peered into different rooms. Rami's heart hammered in his chest. He was certain some kind of security guard was about to pop out. He pictured the security guard looking exactly like Ed, since that was a security guard that he knew. He wondered if this was a failing of his imagination.

"We don't even know if she's in this building," Rami said.

Veda shrugged. She pulled on her backpack straps. "Doesn't hurt to look around. We can at least rule out this building if she's not here."

So, the two of them scouted the halls together. At first, Rami wasn't sure how they would know if the room they were passing was H. F. Bottemtow's, but they quickly discovered that the name of the room's occupant was listed above the door on a whiteboard.

"Candy Mauve," Veda read aloud. "Do you think her first name is Candy or her last name?"

"No idea," Rami was saying when he saw her. He stopped in the middle of the hallway.

"Come on," Veda said.

Rami gestured. Veda followed his pointing. Veda's mouth dropped open into that gape that Rami was getting to know very well.

Standing in the corner of the hallway was Dr. Hale.

And she wasn't alone. Maribeth, her assistant, was right beside her.

Veda grabbed Rami's arm and pulled him down the hallway out of view.

"What is she doing here?" Rami whispered.

"Probably covering up her tracks," Veda said.

"What do you mean?"

"I told you—she stole the painting. And she's here now probably trying to frame H. F. Bottemtow."

"No way." Rami shook his head. He pictured Dr. Hale with her shiny brown loafers. He thought of her gold cat-eye glasses. "I don't think she stole the painting."

"Then why would she be here?" Veda said.

"I don't know," Rami admitted. But he wasn't ready to agree that Dr. Hale was the thief. "Do you think that means H. F. Bottemtow's room is that way, then? That's who she was probably here to see, right?"

Veda nodded. "Good thought. Let's keep looking."

Slowly, and softly, Veda and Rami slunk down the hallway. They continued to read the names on the whiteboards. Finally, they found the whiteboard they were looking for: H. F. Bottemtow.

Except it didn't say H. F. Bottemtow.

It said Hannah Frances Bottemtow.

"Uh, Rami," Veda said after peeking her head in the doorway.

"What?" Rami said. He waited for Veda to tell him that H. F. Bottemtow wasn't there. Or that she looked very angry. Or maybe, just maybe, that the painting was hanging on the wall of the room.

All those potential possibilities made his head spin.

"H. F. Bottemtow doesn't look . . . awake," Veda said quietly.

Rami gulped. "What?"

"Look." Veda motioned toward the door, which she had slightly cracked open.

Taking a deep breath, Rami nudged his head into the doorway. The room was quiet. There was a bed and an empty recliner-type chair that was an ugly shade of gray. On the bed, there was a small elderly woman. And as Veda had reported, this woman looked asleep. Not only that, but this woman was attached to a breathing tube. A monitor at the side of the bed let out a series of beeps.

Rami jumped back into the hallway.

"I don't understand," Rami said. "Was H. F. Bottemtow in an accident? Do you think someone hurt her?"

Veda's eyes widened. "Maybe the person who stole the painting?"

"Maybe," Rami whispered at the exact same time a voice that was not Veda's said, "Rami."

He froze, hoping that if he stayed completely still, he would become truly invisible. It did not work.

"Rami," the voice repeated. "Is that you?"

He knew that voice. It was the voice that sounded like it had received a very fancy education.

Rami's inside-squeezing feeling was back in a big way. He slowly turned around. "Dr. Hale," he said.

In Which They Are Caught

Dr. Hale was dressed in a striped pantsuit. She had on her shiny brown loafers. Her curly gray hair was pinned into a neat bun. Dr. Hale looked calm. Beyond calm. But beside her, Maribeth, her assistant, stood in a more nervous posture.

"Oh wow, oh wow. It is you," Dr. Hale said. "What a surprise." Her eyes turned to Veda. "And who is this?"

Rami opened his mouth, but nothing came out. He knew he had to say something, but he would've really preferred not to.

"I'm Veda," Veda said.

"Yeah, that's Veda," Rami chimed in, finding his voice. "My friend."

Dr. Hale smiled in a way that showed most of her teeth. They looked like tiny daggers, sharp and ready.

"Ah. How nice. And what are you two doing here? Should I infer something from the room you are in front of?"

Rami glanced over his shoulder. They were standing directly in front of H. F. Bottemtow's room. There was no way to deny that.

"We're here to—" Veda started.

"Do you know what happened to her?" Rami said in a steady and clear voice. He looked straight at Dr. Hale—surprising himself, and from the look on her face, surprising her, too. Veda also looked surprised, which gave Rami a new kind of confidence. He pulled back his shoulders.

Dr. Hale shifted her weight from her left foot to her right foot. Rami noticed the leather briefcase she was holding. He didn't think it was big enough to fit *Untitled* inside it. But maybe it was. Could Veda have been right?

"She's sick," Dr. Hale said, and there was a distinct snap to her tone. It made Rami feel like someone had smacked him on the wrist. "She's been in a coma for quite some time. But that's not public knowledge."

"Was she in a coma before the painting went missing?" Veda asked.

"That's classified," Maribeth interjected. She

fiddled with the buttons of her wool cardigan. Her nervous posture looked more nervous-y by the second.

"Thank you, Maribeth," Dr. Hale said. "Maribeth is right. The information is classified. But it's very clear that you two have a keen interest in the case. I can appreciate that." Behind her glasses, her eyes narrowed. "Is there a specific reason you find the case so compelling?"

Veda put her hands on her hips. "The same reason you do, of course."

Dr. Hale let out a sharp laugh. "Oh, I don't believe that's true. I, as you know, am responsible for the institution from which the painting was stolen. That gives me—"

"Motive," Veda said.

"Veda!" Rami hissed. "You can't say that."

"He's right. You really shouldn't say that," Maribeth said. She stopped fiddling with her cardigan's buttons and pointed a long, thin finger at Veda.

Veda, in response, pointed at Dr. Hale. "Do you have the painting in that briefcase?"

Dr. Hale laughed again. Maribeth echoed her, though her laugh was less convincing. "I'm trying to stay good-natured about this," Dr. Hale said. She turned her attention to Rami. "I've always liked you. And I like your sweet mother. She's very kind and has an admirable work ethic. But you have to understand how this doesn't look good. You being here. Especially when the painting went missing while you and your mother were both at the museum."

"Other people were there, too," Veda said. "Including you."

Dr. Hale raised an eyebrow. "I actually was not at the museum at the time of the theft. That's something that hasn't been made public, but I'm happy to share that piece of information with you now."

Rami tried not to look surprised. "Dr. Hale," he began.

"I know, Rami. This is all very unfortunate." She handed Maribeth the briefcase and then dusted her hands. "And as much as I've enjoyed this chat, it's not a good look for any of us to be meeting here. Especially in front of this doorway."

Veda mumbled something. Rami couldn't quite decipher it, but he was pretty sure it wasn't anything nice. He nudged her.

"So as much as it pains me to do this, I must call your mother. I'm guessing she does not know you're here, correct?" Dr. Hale's eyes zeroed in on Rami.

"You don't need to do that," Veda groaned. "Come on."

"Please, Dr. Hale," Rami added.

But Dr. Hale already had her cell phone pressed to her ear, and Rami knew he was about to enter a world of trouble.

A World of Trouble

A world of trouble ended up being an understatement.

Rami's mother was beyond furious. Not only had Dr. Hale, for the time being, banned Rami from coming to the Penelope, but she had also placed Rami's mother on temporary leave. Dr. Hale said that Rami's actions cast a veil of suspicion over the whole family.

"Doesn't Dr. Hale being there make *her* look suspicious?" Rami argued.

"Rami," his mother answered, his name a warning. "I need this job. You know that. What were you thinking?"

He rubbed his temples. "I know—I'm sorry. I really am. We were only trying to help."

He saw something flicker in his mother's eyes. But then they went back to being angry.

"You know, the police discovered something else today," his mother said.

Rami's eyes widened, and he leaned forward with interest. He wished Veda were here. "What?"

"Not only were the cameras turned off, the video footage was edited. Footage was deleted."

Rami processed this. "But why? Why bother only deleting some things and leaving other footage and then turning the cameras all the way off?"

"I don't know," his mom said. "But it's not good. Since I'm the last person seen on camera, it looks like I might have been heading there to adjust the footage."

"Dr. Hale can't really think it's you."

His mom sighed. He noticed dark circles under her eyes, and guilt welled up inside him. He wanted to make it better. He wanted to be able to make her smile like the way she was in the Photo.

"I don't know what she thinks, but your stunt today didn't help. We need to be smart, Rami."

He plopped down on the couch. He rested his elbows on his knees. "I know."

"Do you?" his mom prodded.

"Mom."

"Rami."

They sat in silence for a while. Rami cycled through possible ideas. He didn't think Veda was right about Dr. Hale. But something strange was most certainly going on. And what had happened to H. F. Bottemtow? Had someone hurt her?

On the living room wall, there was a surprise-bird painting hanging. It was the largest one his mom had ever made. He looked at it.

"Mom," he said again.

"Rami," she answered.

He wanted to ask her so many things. He wanted to ask her more about the case. He wanted to tell her how sixth grade had been terrible so far. He wanted to ask her about the mustached guy from the photograph that he had found.

But he couldn't find the words.

So instead he asked, "Why do you hide the birds?"

"What?" she said.

"In your paintings, why do you hide the birds? Like make them hard to find?"

"Oh." She smiled a little, and the sight of her smile made him feel like a crack of sunlight had broken through the cloudy atmosphere of the room. "I don't think of it as hiding them. I've placed them there for you to find. Like a surprise gift. A secret for you to discover. You know that feeling you get when you eventually spot the wing or the talon?"

Rami nodded.

"That's it. That wonderful feeling of having found something? That's what art is about. Making that connection. You're asking someone to see what you see, and also, in the best cases, to maybe find something new."

"Hmm." Rami considered this. "I don't think I really get what you're saying."

His mom leaned over and ruffled his hair. "Yes, you do." She kissed the top of his head. "I'm still mad about what happened today, you know."

"I know," he said.

They sat together on the couch. He went back to trying to find the bird in the painting.

The Phone Rings

He knew his mom was still mad, so he was surprised when the next afternoon she knocked on his door, letting him know Veda was on the phone.

It was the only time this year that someone had called him. He wished it were under better circumstances so he could feel more excited about it. Veda had called his mom's phone—Rami didn't have one of his own.

"Rami?" his mom called out. "Are you coming?"

Rami hopped off his bed and headed for the living room. He took the phone from his mom.

"Hi," he said.

"You in as much trouble as I am?"

"Probably more. My mom's been placed on temporary leave."

He heard Veda exhale through the phone. "Yikes.

What's that mean?" she asked.

"Nothing good."

"Man, I'm sorry."

It was Rami's turn to exhale. "Me too. But it's not your fault. We probably shouldn't have—"

"Nope," Veda interrupted him. "No offense. But that's where you're wrong. We were on the right track. Like, we *are* on the right track. And clearly, I'm right about Dr. Hale."

Rami looked over his shoulder. He expected his mom to be right there, hovering. But she wasn't. The smell of onions sizzling in oil and sumac wafted in from the kitchen, which let him know his mom was cooking. She sometimes did that when she got upset. He pulled the phone closer to his ear.

"Um, I don't know if you are," he finally said. "It seems reasonable she was there—"

"Come on, Rami," Veda interjected. "There's something weird going on. She definitely didn't want us poking around H. F. Bottemtow. Do you think she's the one who hurt H. F. Bottemtow?"

Rami paused for a long time.

"Rami?" Veda said.

"Yeah. I'm here. I'm just thinking . . . Why would Dr. Hale hurt H. F. Bottemtow?"

"Because H. F. Bottemtow knew the truth! That Dr. Hale stole the painting."

"Uh," Rami said. His stomach rumbled as the smells from the kitchen grew stronger. It felt weird to be hungry at a time like this. But he couldn't help it. It smelled so good. "I don't know if that really tracks."

Veda made a clicking noise with her tongue. "Okay, okay. Maybe that's not exactly how the pieces fit together. But something is up with Dr. Hale. We know that for sure. And she knows that we know that. That's why she's trying to block us."

Rami sighed. "She's been pretty effective at blocking us. It's not like we can go to the Penelope now. Which is really bad news because I feel like we need to talk to Blue again."

"We do need to talk to Blue again," Veda agreed.

"But we can't. Because Blue is at the Penelope. And I'm not allowed at the Penelope. There's no way Ed or Theodore will let us through the front door."

"That's why we're not going to go through the front door. We're going to sneak in. Meet me there tonight at ten."

"Veda! Have you lost your mind? We can't sneak into the Penelope. There are alarms and . . ." Rami didn't exactly know how the security system worked, but he assumed it was complicated. "Plus, ten p.m.? How am I supposed to get out of my apartment? I can't believe my mom is letting me talk to you on the phone. She's never going to—"

"Rami, we have to do this now. It's Thursday. Spring break is almost over."

He thought about this for a moment. "I don't think spring break being almost over is our biggest problem."

"It might not be the biggest, but it is a problem. Less free time to investigate. Recycling club is going to keep me really busy once we get back to school."

"Uh, I'm not sure—"

"Rami, I'll see you there," Veda said. "Ten p.m., sharp."

And then she hung up the phone.

The Turtle Is Drawing

It took the girl now named Blue a moment to recognize what the turtle was doing.

"Are you drawing?" Blue whispered as she looked out the hallway window.

The turtle, of course, did not answer. This is a story with lots of mysterious and strange things, but it is not a story that features a turtle who can speak with humans.

The girl floated closer to the window. She strained her eyes to get a better view.

The turtle was drawing. Or, rather, the turtle was moving around in a patch of mud, making an outline with her feet.

It very much seemed like the turtle was drawing.

"What are you making?" Blue said. This time she did not whisper.

But the turtle still did not answer.

Blue watched and watched. The turtle moved quite slow. She was, after all, a turtle.

But then—Blue saw something in what the turtle had created.

"I know that face," Blue said.

She floated down the hallway, back into Cherry Hall. And then she turned around and floated out of Cherry Hall, returning to the hallway window. She looked at the turtle's artwork again.

"I've seen you," she said, staring at the turtle's drawing.

She knew she had seen the face recently.

But there was something else. Deep down, she knew that face belonged to someone who had been important to her.

Who was still important to her.

"Who are you?" Blue said.

It was a question that had many answers.

26

A Question, and Possibly an Answer

Agatha noticed that the girl in the window was watching her.

She was happy about it.

After that woman had shown her the drawing, Agatha had become interested in making her own art. She had started to make drawings in the mud and in the grass. But hardly any humans ever noticed.

The girl in the window was noticing, though. Agatha could tell.

She could also tell that the girl in the window was asking a question.

The drawing the woman had once made of Agatha had asked a question. But it had answered a question, too.

Art, Agatha understood, was made of both

questions and answers.

Agatha continued to draw.

Look, Agatha was trying to say with her drawing.

Pay attention.

Remember.

Sneaking Out

Rami figured there must be some law of the universe that every footstep you take after bedtime makes a louder sound than any movement you make during the day.

It was only a few feet from his bedroom to the back door of his apartment, but with each groaning step, he was sure his mom would wake up. And it would all be over.

I can't believe I'm doing this, he thought.

This is such a bad idea.

He took one deep breath after another. And he sweated. But he kept moving, one creaking footstep after the other.

When he finally reached the door, he pulled the knob slowly. It whined. He held his breath. He waited. His mother didn't come.

He slipped out the door, closed it, and pressed his back against it. Deep breaths.

Creeping down the outside stairwell, he moved as quickly as he could. *I'm doing this*, he thought. *I'm really sneaking out.*

It was going okay. It was going great. His heart thumped in his chest. But once he reached the bottom step, he took the next turn too widely and bumped into the dumpster.

"Oof," he said.

But then he noticed a stray piece of paper drifting up from the dumpster. It was a receipt.

He bent over and picked up the paper. He was about to toss it back in the dumpster until he saw the words at the top.

Evergreen Pines Cafeteria.

Someone who lived in his building had recently gone to Evergreen Pines. They had purchased a bottle of water, a bag of potato chips, and a candy bar.

He held his breath. He considered the possibilities. He knew there must be many, but there was only one that kept popping up in his brain.

28 The Darkness

"People online say there's a secret passageway" was the first thing Veda said when Rami arrived.

Rami, though, barely heard her. The whole walk to the Penelope, he'd heard his heartbeat in his ears.

He'd shoved the receipt into the pocket of his coat. It sat there like a wrinkled grenade.

Who had visited Evergreen Pines?

His first thought was Theodore. Or, at least, he wanted it to be Theodore. He didn't want to consider the other person it could be. The person he kept picturing in his mind.

He pulled the receipt out of his pocket. His heart tumbled when he saw the time stamp on it. His mom didn't work then, but Theodore did.

She would've been free to visit Evergreen Pines without anyone noticing her absence.

He swallowed. It couldn't be his mom, right?

If she'd visited Evergreen Pines, did she know about H. F. Bottemtow being so sick? And worse, did she have something to do with H. F. Bottemtow's bad condition?

No way. The answer had to be no way.

But a voice kept nagging at Rami.

He thought about his mom. Who loved art. Who chose to surround herself with it. Who was always looking for it.

But almost no one who visited the Penelope ever noticed her. Knew that she was a part of the reason they were able to enjoy the art. The reason they were able to see beautiful things in a beautiful place.

The sound of his own heartbeat grew louder.

"Rami!" Veda said. She didn't even bother to whisper. "Did you hear what I said? I think there's a secret passageway into the museum."

Rami ran his fingers over the crumpled paper. He knew he had a choice to make. If he showed this to Veda, there was no going back. She would begin to suspect his mom, too.

"Veda," he said slowly.

"Where do you think it is?"

"What?"

"The secret passageway."

"Veda, I don't think there is any secret passageway." He stared up at the Penelope. In the darkness, it seemed bigger. Less like an old house, and more like an institution. He wondered what it was about the darkness that made things seem larger. More imposing.

Did the darkness make you see things differently? Was it sometimes hardest to see what was right in front of your face?

"It's a really old house. It stands to reason that—"

Rami interrupted her. "If there ever was a secret passageway, don't you think they got rid of it when they converted the house into a museum?"

The wind blew, and Rami shivered. He was glad that he had remembered his coat. Even if he'd initially worn it to disguise the fact he was still in his pajamas. He'd almost changed, but then he thought wearing his pajamas was a good cover in case his mom caught him before he'd managed to sneak out.

But now he was in his pajamas. About to illegally break into an art museum. Which probably meant he was about to go to jail. He couldn't decide whether it was a blessing or curse to be hauled away to jail in your pajamas. There was a certain degree of comfort, but also a large potential dose of embarrassment.

"I think every old house has secrets. And we just have to figure out the Penelope's."

Veda paced around the side of the building. Rami followed her. They made their way into the back garden. Rami had always liked the back garden. It was peaceful. And in the summer, he would sometimes sit out here and read while his mom worked.

He was thinking about the garden in the summertime, imagining warm sunlight on his face and a feeling of calm, when Veda grabbed his shoulder.

"Rami!" she said.

He went back to shivering. The daydream about summer warmth and calm was gone. "What?"

She pointed to the window. "Look! It's Blue!"

Veda waved while Rami squinted at the window. He could make out a shadowy figure. He blinked a few times, and the figure's face came into better view. Veda was right. Blue was standing by the window. Or, to be precise, she was floating.

Rami shivered again.

"Can you hear us?" Veda shouted at the window.

"Veda," Rami whispered with force.

"What?"

"I don't think we should be so loud. Someone might hear us."

Veda made a show of looking all around the garden. "No one is here. Except Blue. And she's who we want to talk to, right?" Then Veda stared at the ground. "You think I'm too noisy."

"No," Rami said softly. "I get why you were shouting, but . . . there might be cameras. Or something? Like maybe we're being recorded?"

Veda frowned. She tugged on her knitted hat. It was light pink with a rainbow pom-pom on top. Rami hadn't seen it before. He wondered how her mom could possibly knit so many hats.

"Hmm," Veda said slowly. "If we're being recorded, we might as well make the most of our time here, right?"

Veda was brave. She always spoke up. It made Rami want to be brave, too. Rami wanted to tell her that. But he wasn't sure how. So instead, he decided he would tell her the truth.

Rami reached into his pocket and pulled out the piece of paper. "Veda. Look at this."

Veda took the paper out of his hands. "What's this?" She peered at it. "A receipt?"

"Look at it," Rami said.

"Oh," Veda said. "It's from Evergreen Pines. Did you buy something there?"

"It's from the cafeteria," Rami said. "Someone

visited there. They bought a water, a bag of chips, and a candy bar."

"Yes," Veda said slowly. "I assume lots of people visit there, right? To, like, get food while they are there to see their family members? And there's nothing weird about buying a bag of chips. Or a candy bar."

Rami shook his head. "You're not understanding."

"I know," Veda said. "I'm really not."

"I found this receipt in the dumpster of my apartment building."

Veda wrinkled her nose. "You dug through the dumpster?"

Rami shook his head again. "Veda, no. I—"

"Oh!" Veda said. "You think this means your mom visited Evergreen Pines."

"Yeah," Rami said. He looked down at the sneakers his mom had bought him. The sneakers she'd spent her whole bonus on. The ones that didn't quite fit anymore. "I don't know."

"It doesn't necessarily mean anything," Veda said softly.

"I think it might," Rami said. "It's even stamped with a time when I know she was off work. She could have definitely visited then."

Veda exhaled loudly. "Well, we should talk to Blue. That's what we're here to do, right?"

Rami stared at the window. The shadowy figure was still there. "How? She probably won't be able to hear us through the glass."

"I have an idea."

Rami groaned. "Don't tell me it has to do with secret passageways. I'm telling you, I don't think those—"

"No," Veda said, a giant grin spreading across her face. "But do you see that bench over there?"

In Which They Reach the Window

While Rami was pushing the bench across the courtyard, he kept thinking about going to jail in his pajamas. He'd decided that in the end he would probably be happy to be wearing something comfy.

"We're definitely going to jail," he mumbled as he kept pushing the bench.

"Only if they catch us," Veda said brightly.

"How are you not winded?"

"It's not that big of a bench."

"It's heavy!" Rami said in between huffs of breath.

"Stop complaining," Veda said. "And keep pushing."

So, he did. And eventually, they managed to move the bench from its original spot all the way over to below the window.

"Now what?" Rami said. "Even if we stand on the bench, we aren't going to be tall enough to reach the window."

Veda's wide grin appeared again. She had a very elastic smile. "I know. But I'll be tall enough if I can get on your shoulders."

"What?" Rami felt a little bit panicky. "I don't think that's a great idea."

"Oh, come on. I did gymnastics when I was younger. It'll be easy. Lean down. Unless you want to get on my shoulders?"

Rami weighed his choices. Neither of them seemed like good ones. But he was also outside an art museum in the middle of the night, freezing in his pajamas. This wasn't exactly a night that was filled with great options.

"Fine. I'll hoist you up," Rami finally said. "But don't wiggle a lot. I don't want to lose my balance."

"Okay, okay," Veda said. "I got it. Don't worry."

"What's the opposite of 'don't worry'? That's what I am right now," Rami said, but Veda wasn't listening. She had already jumped onto his back and was hoisting herself up onto his shoulders.

"Try to stand still," Veda said.

"I'm trying." His knees knocked together as he

tried to keep his balance. He was certain he was going to fall over.

"Rami."

"Veda," he replied.

"Try harder, okay?"

"Okay." He swallowed and took a deep breath. He steadied himself and then grabbed her ankles. Both for her safety and to ease his nerves.

"Hi, Blue!" Veda said.

"Can you see her?" Rami asked.

"Yeah," Veda said. "But I can't hear her. The glass is too thick."

"Ugh," Rami said. "I don't know how much longer I can stand like this." He made the mistake of looking down, which made him nervous. And dizzy. He wobbled a little bit.

"Hold on. I think she's saying something. I'm trying to read her lips. Are you saying 'drawing'?"

"Me?" Rami said. He could feel sweat collecting on his forehead. His ankles bent, making him sway from side to side. "I did not say 'drawing.'"

"Not you! Blue," Veda said. "I think she's saying 'drawing.'"

Rami thought about it. "Do you think she could be talking about the receipt?"

"I doubt it. Does 'receipt' sound like 'drawing'?"

"No, but . . ."

"Wait! She's saying something else," Veda said. "'Mud'?"

"'Mud'?" Rami said.

"'Mud,' and maybe 'turtle.'"

"'Mud, and maybe turtle'?"

"No, 'mud' and 'turtle' and 'drawing.'"

"That's what I said," Rami said, shifting uncomfortably, trying to keep his balance.

"You said 'maybe turtle.'"

"You said 'maybe turtle'!"

"Okay, okay," Veda said. "Well, I am pretty sure she is saying some combination of 'drawing,' 'mud,' and 'turtle.'"

"That doesn't make any sense. Are you sure she isn't saying 'receipt'?"

"Pretty sure. You are obsessed with that."

Rami considered this. Maybe he was obsessed with the receipt. But it seemed like an important clue. "Can you at least ask her about it?"

"It's worth a shot, I guess. Hand it to me," Veda said.

"I don't know if I can do that without us both falling over."

"Rami! Try!"

Rami took another deep breath. He dug in his pocket and pulled out the receipt. He wobbled again, but he caught his balance. He handed it to her.

"Evergreen Pines," he heard Veda say. "This is a receipt from there. Do you know about Evergreen Pines?"

"What's she saying?" Rami asked. "Is she answering you?"

"She's shaking her head," Veda said. "I don't think she knows anything about the receipt. She keeps pointing to the corner of the courtyard and saying 'drawing' and 'mud' and 'turtle.' Do you see a turtle anywhere?"

Instinctively, Rami turned to look at the corner of the courtyard. But the second he turned, he knew he'd made a mistake. He felt his balance shift.

But it was too late to correct it.

He and Veda both tumbled onto the bench. As his knee collided with the hard surface, he let out a yelp.

And then the courtyard floodlights came on.

After the Tumble

Agatha watched the two kids move the bench across the courtyard. She recognized the boy. He often came to the courtyard.

She had a particular affection for him. Because of whom he was related to. It is very easy for turtles to notice patterns of relation between humans. She was certain that he was connected to the woman who had drawn her.

As Agatha watched the kids climb up onto the bench, and the girl hop onto the boy's shoulders, she knew it was not a good idea. It looked very unsteady. She wished that she had a way to warn them.

Humans might not think of turtles as curious or wise creatures. They tend to tell stories about curious cats. Wise owls.

But turtles are both curious and wise. Or at least Agatha was.

She listened as the kids in the courtyard tried to decode what the girl in the window was telling them. The girl whose eyes had something in them that Agatha recognized. A question. A question that Agatha believed she could answer.

Look, Agatha thought. *Look at what I've drawn.*

She saw the boy turn.

Yes, she thought. *You're looking in the right direction now.*

But then they fell. A loud crash.

Bright lights flooded the garden.

Agatha knew she should go deeper into her burrow. But she couldn't help herself. She wanted to see if they would see what she had made.

She needed to.

The boy and the girl scrambled. There was shouting.

But then the boy saw it.

"Look," the boy said.

Yes, Agatha thought. *Look*.

The Picture in the Mud

Rami knew that he should run.

The garden that had been dark moments ago was now flooded with light. This signaled that someone was here. It would not be good if the guards, especially Ed, found them here. It would not be good at all.

But his feet stopped when he saw it. It was a drawing. Maybe. It looked like someone had taken a stick and etched in the mud. Some of the drawing had been smudged, washed away by either rain or footprints. Possibly both. But there was still enough of it left for Rami to recognize it.

He stared at the face that had been drawn in the mud. And it stared back at him. He saw the bushy eyebrows. He recognized those bushy eyebrows.

"I know you," he whispered.

"Rami!" Veda shouted. "We need to get out of here!"

"Veda—you need to look at this."

Veda hesitated. She was near the exit. But she didn't leave him. She turned and walked back to where he was standing, neck bent, staring at the mud.

"There's a picture here. Someone drew a face."

Veda stood next to him. She was breathing quickly. "Okay, so we found the drawing in the mud. But where's the turtle?" Veda said. The air around them was damp and cold. The kind that chills your bones.

Rami wasn't sure about the turtle. But he felt like he could both laugh and cry. Cry from how cold he felt. How certain he was that they were going to be caught. All the trouble that he knew was heading their way.

And laugh. Laugh because of this picture in the mud. And how he knew who it was. Even if he didn't understand who drew it or why.

Also, he was probably going to end up in jail in his pajamas.

He let out a sound. It was somewhere between a laugh and cry.

"Is that a face?" Veda was squinting at the mud.

Rami could hear a ticking clock in his head. He

knew something was about to happen. There was a countdown. He just didn't know what it was to yet.

"It is. And I know whose face it is."

Veda kept staring at it. "It's not Blue's. That's for sure. Do you think she drew it?" Veda looked up at the window. With the bright lights on, it was harder to see if Blue was still there. "Wait! Is there a turtle over there? I'm going to go see—"

"Hey!" a voice that was not Veda's shouted, interrupting her.

It was deep and gruff.

Rami knew it belonged to Ed.

"Run," he whispered to Veda. And they both took off.

"Rami!" he heard Ed shouting. "Is that you? I know it's you!"

Rami's heart pounded in his chest. But he kept running. Running away from the mud and toward the face that was drawn in it.

In Which They Try to Put the Pieces Together

Once they had rounded a few blocks, Veda slowed down.

Rami bent over and pushed his hands against his knees. His lungs burned. He wasn't sure he'd ever catch his breath again.

"He saw you," Veda said.

"He . . . did?" Rami managed to get out as he gasped for air.

"That was the security guard, yeah? What's his name?"

"Ed," Rami answered. He looked around. He wasn't familiar with the street they were on. He'd just run as fast as he could in the quickest direction. Though as he looked around some more, he spotted a building in the distance that he recognized. It had a copper-shingled roof. That made it unusual. So, Rami remembered it. His pulse slowed as he decided he could make his way home from here.

They were in a neighborhood made up mostly of big old houses. Ones like the Victorian mansion of the Penelope. Houses that had wide porches and turrets and shiny glass-paned doors. The large houses cast shadows across the sidewalk, shadows that felt a bit menacing when Rami looked at them for too long.

"That's a problem, right? That Ed saw us?" Veda said. She paced up and down the sidewalk. "We have a lot of problems. Like I don't know what that drawing was supposed to be?"

"I do," Rami said. "Or I think I do."

Veda stared at him. The streetlamp above illuminated her face, which was filled with confusion.

"I saw it," Rami explained. "I mean, I know what whoever drew it was trying to show."

"And what's that?"

"It's the other security guard," Rami said, his words slow but purposeful. The sky overhead glowed purple, the darkness mixing with the lamplight. "My neighbor."

"Your neighbor?"

"Theodore D. Cornell."

Veda wrinkled her nose some more. She shuffled her feet on the sidewalk. "Wait. It was the security guard? What does that mean?"

Rami's face flushed. He felt cold but also sweaty. "I'm not sure exactly. I mean, of the two security guards, I would've thought Ed seemed more likely."

Veda rubbed her temples. "I'm so confused. Are you saying it's Ed or Theodore?"

"I'm saying I saw Theodore's picture in the mud. And Theodore is my upstairs neighbor. He sometimes returns our mail when it gets delivered to him by mistake."

"Sorry, I'm not following here. No offense, but just because he's your neighbor, that doesn't make him an art thief." Veda pulled her knitted hat down farther over her ears. She was shivering, too. "And did you really see his picture in the mud? Wasn't that just . . . mud?"

Rami knew they needed to go somewhere, get out of the cold. But the question was where should they go? And Rami was still sorting through the pieces, trying to make them fit.

"Theodore works at the museum," Rami finally said, trying to make sense of everything. "And Blue wanted us to see that drawing of him. It was a drawing. I know it was."

He kept visualizing that face. The one that he had seen in the mud.

Blue had pointed to the mud face drawing. Blue wanted them to see it.

The sound of Veda's voice broke his concentration. "Do you think Ed is still looking for us? Like, what are the chances he's called our parents?" Veda gulped. Rami was used to being the one who swallowed, but he could see the nervousness written all over her face. "Or worse, do you think he called the police?"

"Probably," Rami admitted.

Veda looked at the ground. "Maybe we should go home, Rami. I don't think we should mess with another security guard. Ed is already out to get us. Do we want to make the other one mad, too? That seems . . . scary."

"But what if he stole the painting?"

Veda didn't look up. "Maybe he did. But I'm not sure we'll be able to prove it. What if—"

"I need to solve this," Rami blurted out.

This made Veda look up. "I know you want to solve it, Rami. I do, too. But . . . I don't know—"

"No, you don't get it. I mean, I really need this," Rami said.

Veda gave him a questioning look.

He ran his cold hand through his hair. "Look, my mom's in trouble. And I need to help her. But also, everyone thinks I'm a loser. And I'm . . . I'm so tired of feeling like they're right."

His heart hammered. The words he'd spoken hung in the air like thick smoke. He couldn't believe he'd said those words, but he also couldn't believe he'd kept it all inside for this long.

"No, they don't," Veda said quickly.

"Yes, they do. You remember what my friends did to me."

"Yeah, but those guys are jerks. You have other friends."

Rami shook his head.

"Yes. You do."

He hung his head. "No one talks to me at school. I'm invisible."

"Well, you don't ever talk to anyone."

Rami frowned. "That's . . ."

"It's true. You don't."

"That's because . . ." He couldn't find the words. He didn't know how to tell her that Matty and him had become friends in kindergarten when he'd found Matty crying because one of the other kids had stolen Matty's favorite toy. Rami had helped him get it back. Matty had listened when Rami had told him everything he knew about tigers. They'd geeked out over wildlife facts together. And the next year, they'd met Henry. They'd all gone as matching knights for Halloween in second grade, and race car drivers in third grade. They'd played endless hours of video games and had spent the summers riding bikes up and down the cul-de-sac near Henry's house.

But then at the start of sixth grade, it was like suddenly everything Rami did was wrong. His friends made faces when he talked. They'd pretend not to see him when they saw him walking down the hall. It was like he no longer fit, but he didn't know why.

And how that feeling, that feeling of not fitting, had made him start to wonder about his dad. He knew those things weren't connected. But it felt like they were. Like something was deeply wrong with him. Like everyone would always leave him behind. Reject him.

Like he would never fit.

But Rami didn't say that. He didn't say anything.

As he stood in silence, he looked at Veda's face. And he saw something that surprised him. Something that made him think that someday—not tonight, but someday—he might be able to tell her. And that maybe, just maybe, she would understand.

Veda walked closer to him. "Hey," she said, gently elbowing him in the side. "I already told you once, but I'll say it again: you're not invisible. I see you."

"Veda," he finally said. "I really need to solve this case."

"*We* need to solve this case," Veda replied.

"You want to quit, though," Rami said.

"I don't want to quit," Veda said. "I'm just kind of scared."

Rami's eyes widened with surprise. "Scared? Of getting in trouble?"

"Of not being able to solve it. I've been waiting my whole life for a moment like this. But maybe I'm all talk, you know. Like the type of person who listens to podcasts, but not the type of person ever featured on one."

Rami raised his eyebrows. "You've been waiting your whole life for the Penelope to get robbed?"

Veda shook her head, laughing slightly. "No. But, like . . . to get to have a big adventure. To solve my first case. And now I'm a little worried that I don't have what it takes."

"You definitely have what it takes."

Veda looked at him and smiled. "You know what? You're right. We're going to solve this."

"You really think so?"

"Yup," she said. "Because I'm a good friend." She smiled wider. "Can you at least admit that? Or do I have to keep begging you?"

It was Rami's turn to laugh. "Okay, okay."

"Say it."

"What?"

"That we're friends. And that I'm a good friend at that."

He laughed some more. "You're a good friend, Veda."

Veda nodded approvingly, grinning from ear to ear. "And I don't talk too much, yeah?"

"You talk a lot." Rami gave her a teasing smile. "Which is the exact right amount for you."

"Perfect answer," Veda said. "Now, let's solve this thing."

"Okay. I think we should go to Theodore's apartment."

"I don't know—"

"I saw his picture in the mud," Rami said. He knew what he'd seen. And once you've seen something, you can't unsee it. "I know what I saw, and Blue must've seen it, too. That's why she was pointing over there."

"Or she was pointing at the turtle," Veda said.

"The turtle?" Rami hadn't noticed the turtle. Only the etching. But Veda had gotten a glimpse of Agatha, right before Ed caught them in the courtyard.

"It was him," Rami said again. "I know it was. But what I can't figure out is who drew it."

"Maybe the turtle?" Veda offered.

Rami shook his head. "Turtles don't draw."

"And ghost girls don't randomly appear in art museums," Veda countered.

"True, but here we are," Rami said.

"Here we are," Veda repeated. "I think that could be a good catchphrase. If I end up making a podcast about this."

"Veda," Rami said.

"Sorry, sorry, getting ahead of myself," Veda said. She rubbed her hands together.

"So should we do it?" Rami shifted his weight from his right foot to his left. "Head to my apartment building and knock on Theodore's door and ask him—"

"Isn't it the middle of the night?" Veda said.

"Yeah." Rami looked up at the night sky. He

wished, not for the first time, that the lights from the city of Maple Lake didn't blot out the stars. But they did. Yet, he knew that somewhere up there, stars were shining. Even if he couldn't see them. "It is the middle of the night. But that's kind of a good thing."

Veda's smile turned sly. "Catch him off guard?"

Rami matched his smile to hers. "Exactly. Catch the security guard off guard."

"We should ask him if he knows Blue," Veda interjected. "I think that's a good place to start."

"But how will he know who we're talking about?"

Veda paused for a moment. "Can you draw her?"

Rami bit his lip. "I don't really draw . . . that's more my mom's thing."

"I saw you drawing once," Veda said.

"What?"

"In class."

Rami swallowed. "I guess I doodle a little . . . sometimes."

"Can you try?" Veda pressed.

He didn't have any paper with him. Only the receipt. And he didn't have a pen.

"I don't have a pen."

"I do." Veda pulled one from her pocket.

"You're prepared," Rami said, smiling slightly.

"I always am."

Rami sat down on the sidewalk. He thought about what his mom had said. About how art was about making a connection, about not only sharing what you see, but inviting someone else to find what they can see.

He fiddled with the pen and pictured Blue. Finally, he began to draw.

When he was done, he showed it to Veda.

"It's her," Veda said.

Wings, Rami thought, picturing his mom's bird paintings. *You see it.*

Theodore D. Cornell

Rami braced for his apartment building to be surrounded when they got there. He was expecting flashing lights, swirls of red from sirens. But there was none of that.

The night sky was dark. And everything was quiet and still. Except for the wind that rustled the bare branches of the trees.

He and Veda crept up the back outdoor metal steps. The steps let out an occasional whine underneath their feet, which would cause them both to freeze. They'd wait for a few moments and then begin the climb again.

"Maybe we should've risked using the inside entrance," Rami whispered. "It might freak him out that we're at his back door."

"It's the middle of the night. He's going to be

freaked out no matter what," Veda said.

Rami took a deep breath once they reached the back door of Theodore D. Cornell's apartment. But he did not swallow. He looked at Veda and lifted his fist, knocking loudly three times.

"I don't know if that was loud enough to wake him up," Veda said. She added a few knocks of her own. She was a much louder knocker than Rami.

While she was in the process of beating on his door, the door cracked open.

"Hello?" a groggy voice said.

Rami looked at Veda. Veda looked at Rami.

It was Veda who found her words first. "Do you know Blue?" she said.

"Who?" The voice was thick with sleep. The door was still only open a sliver. "Who are you? What do you want? It's the crack of dawn."

"Technically, I don't think dawn is cracking yet," Veda said.

"Rami? Is that you?" Theodore asked.

Rami shoved the receipt with the drawing of Blue through the open sliver. "This is Blue. Do you know her?"

There was a long pause. Rami was used to waiting out silences.

Veda, on the other hand, wanted to fill it. "We

saw your face. Or at least Rami did. And I saw a turtle. Do you know the turtle?"

The door swung all the way open. Theodore D. Cornell was standing there in bright orange striped pajamas, and what was left of his hair was standing up on the top of his head.

"Pajama party," Rami said weakly, pointing at his own pajama pants. Theodore D. Cornell did not seem amused. "Uh—"

"Ah, come on in. Get out of the cold," Theodore said as he motioned for Rami and Veda to step through the door.

Veda and Rami exchanged glances. There was inherent danger implied when you decided to walk straight into a stranger's house.

"What are you waiting for? Wasn't I supposed to invite you in? That's what you were angling for, yes?" Theodore said. His voice was still groggy, but it was also impatient.

Rami looked at Veda again. And Veda looked at Rami. Slowly, Rami stepped inside, and Veda followed him.

Theodore's apartment wasn't so different from Rami's. The layout was practically the same. Theodore led them into the living area, where he took a seat in an overstuffed recliner. Veda and Rami sat down on the sofa across from him. The room was tidy, the coffee table empty except for one water glass and a few fingerprint smudges.

Theodore leaned back in the recliner. His forehead wrinkled with thought, but he didn't say anything.

Veda cleared her throat. "Do you know Blue?"

"You already asked that. I don't know who Blue is."

"Blue is her." Rami pointed at the drawing he'd made on the back of the receipt. He looked down at Blue's face. Her eyes were almost exactly the same way they were in *Untitled*. He felt proud of that.

Theodore shook his head, letting out a sharp bark of a laugh. "That's not Blue. That's Hannah."

"Hannah?" A rush of recognition ran through Rami. "Like H. F. Bottemtow Hannah?"

Theodore made a muttering sound. "Ah, yeah. H. F. That's H. F. But you know that, right? Isn't that what you're doing, just copying the painting?"

"No," Rami said, but before he could explain more, Veda interjected.

"But H. F. is an old lady. She's sick. We saw her."

Theodore leaned forward. "You saw her?"

"At Evergreen Pines. She looked really sick," Veda said. "Speaking of Evergreen Pines, this is a receipt from Evergreen Pines. Rami found it here. Have you been there?"

Theodore pinched the bridge of his nose and sighed. "She is sick. She's very, very ill."

"You didn't answer my question," Veda said. "Have you been there?"

"What happened to her?" Rami said.

Theodore waved his hand in the air. His lips made a sputtering sound like he was saying many things at once. None of them decipherable. "Wait. What are you doing here? I don't know why I let you in. It's the middle of the night—"

"You said Blue was Hannah," Veda said. There was a spark in her voice. She'd caught fire with an idea. Veda snatched the receipt from Rami. She pointed at it. "You said that this is Hannah?"

"Yup. That's her from when she was younger."

"We saw her," Veda said. "We've seen her."

"At Evergreen Pines?"

"No," Veda said. "Not the old lady. This Hannah." Veda pointed at the receipt again.

Theodore's eyes went wide. "What? How is that possible? Where?"

"At the museum," Veda said.

Theodore shook his head. "That can't be right.

I thought I was imagining her when I saw her . . . but . . ."

"You saw her there, too?" Veda asked. "At the museum?"

"We also saw your face," Rami interjected. He felt like he needed to add something. But he wasn't quite sure if it was the right thing to say.

Theodore turned to Rami. "You saw my face?"

"Yes. We think a turtle drew it," Veda explained.

"Actually, we aren't sure about the turtle part," Rami clarified.

Theodore's face crumpled with confusion. His eyes looked bleary. He rubbed them. "I don't know what I was thinking, letting you in here. I just got startled when I saw that drawing of her. It brought back . . ."

Now it was Rami's turn to feel a spark. "It brought back a memory for you, didn't it? You knew her." Rami looked at the receipt. "That was your receipt that I found, wasn't it? You've been going to Evergreen Pines. You've been visiting H. F. I thought it couldn't have been your receipt because it was during your work hours at the museum. But it was you. Wasn't it?"

As he processed everything, a ping of guilt mixed

with relief washed over him. He shouldn't have ever doubted his mother. It hadn't been her receipt. She wasn't secretly visiting H. F. Bottemtow. It wasn't her. It'd never been her.

Theodore shook his head over and over again. "I'm too tired. I don't know why I said that. It's been a bad couple of weeks." He stood up. "You should go."

"You said you saw her," Veda said. "And we've seen her, too."

"I don't know what you're talking about," Theodore said.

"Yes, you do."

He kept shaking his head.

"Maybe you should drink some water," Veda offered. "My mom always says to drink water when you feel tired. Tiredness is often just dehydration."

"It's the middle of the night," Theodore said.

Veda pushed the water glass toward him. "Yes. And you're tired."

He sat back down. "You kids are something," Theodore said, but he did reach for the water glass.

"You've been visiting her at Evergreen Pines," Rami said, repeating his theory. "Did you know her?"

"Hannah?" Theodore said. "I knew her. A long time ago."

There was something in Theodore's voice that Rami recognized. A missing. A sadness. A loneliness.

He thought of Blue.

"Blue is Hannah," Rami whispered.

"Blue is Hannah," Veda repeated. She held up the painting again. "This is Hannah, right?"

Theodore nodded solemnly. "That's what she looked like when we first met."

Veda's eyes narrowed with interest. Rami could feel the beams of excitement radiating off her. "You knew her when she was young?"

"She was my best friend," Theodore said.

"So . . ." Rami breathed out. His brain was spinning. "The girl in the painting—that's Hannah. She painted herself?"

Theodore nodded again.

"Wait," Veda said. She jumped to her feet. "That means Blue isn't a ghost."

"Then what is she?" Rami asked.

"I don't know, but if Hannah is still alive—" Veda stopped talking. She looked nervously in Theodore's direction.

Theodore hung his head. He stared down at his hands. "Hannah is very sick. She's in a coma. The doctors don't know if she will ever wake up."

"We need to go see her. Maybe we can help," Veda said.

"Help?" Rami said. "You mean go back to the museum?"

Theodore frowned. "What are you talking about? She's not at the museum."

"She is," Veda and Rami said in unison.

"I mean," Rami explained, "we saw her. This version of her." He pointed at his drawing of Blue. "And you just said that you saw her, too."

"I hallucinated her." He rubbed his eyes. "I can't trust my mind these days."

"It wasn't your mind. She's there. We've seen her," Veda said.

"That's impossible."

Rami shrugged. "I guess it is. But it's also true."

Theodore frowned some more. Rami was getting the impression that Theodore mostly made grumpy expressions. He looked around the room. It was strange to him that so little hung on Theodore's walls. Only a circular mirror that looked like the type of mirror that might have been hanging there before Theodore even moved in.

"You sketch well," Theodore said. "In your drawing, she really looks like how I remember her."

Theodore kicked himself back in the recliner. It made a squeaking noise as it moved. "I've been trying to help her to remember herself. The doctors said that if we have any hope of her waking up, she needs to remember herself. Some gibberish like that. I keep trying to help her, but I'm not sure anything is working." He picked up the receipt. "Can I have this?"

"Hands off. It's evidence," Veda said.

Theodore's face moved into an expression somewhere between amusement and agitation.

Rami replayed Theodore's compliment of his drawing. He felt a surge of pride that Theodore wanted to keep it. Theodore had found something meaningful in it, a discovery, a remembrance.

And then it clicked.

"That's why you stole the painting," Rami said, the spark from before catching fire inside his brain.

Theodore's face drained of color. Veda's head jerked toward Rami.

"Rami," Veda hissed. "You can't just accuse someone of that."

"I'm right. Aren't I?" Rami said, standing up. "You took the painting. But not because you wanted to sell it or anything like that. Because you wanted to show it to her. Because you wanted her to—"

"Remember," Theodore filled in. He sighed.

The room was quiet for a while. Neither Rami nor Veda quite knew what to do with an admitted art thief in their presence.

Rami began to pace. He circled the glass coffee table. He admired the cleanliness of Theodore's freshly vacuumed carpet. There was an energy inside him that made him feel like he could leap and touch the ceiling.

Eventually, Rami broke the silence. "You knew all the security codes because you work at the Penelope. Were you the one that turned off the cameras?"

Theodore didn't answer for a while. Finally, he spoke. "I'll tell you everything if you—"

"We can't promise not to tell anyone," Veda interrupted. "We're kind of in a whole bunch of trouble."

Rami, of course, thought of his mother. And how this would exonerate her.

"No, no. I understand," Theodore said, and his voice made it sound like he actually did. "I just feel like I need to explain myself."

And so, Theodore told them the story.

Theodore's Story

There was once a boy who met the young girl who sketched every day at the edge of her parents' apple orchard.

(You know this already. But sometimes it's helpful to be reminded.)

This boy became a young man who was friends with the young girl who became a young woman who sketched every day.

This young woman left their small town. But before she left, she gave the young man a gift.

A painting.

A painting without a name.

The young man did have a name, though. It was Theodore D. Cornell.

The young woman also had a name. It was Hannah Frances Bottemtow.

While Hannah traveled far and wide, Theodore stayed in Maple Lake. Because he missed Hannah, and also because he needed a job, he started to work at the Penelope L. Brooks Museum. He was the security guard.

But because he was the security guard, he got to be around paintings all day. The paintings made him feel less lonely. The paintings reminded him of Hannah.

Back at his apartment, he had hung the untitled painting on his wall. It was the only thing he had hung up. He would look at it and think about how it was just as good as the paintings in the Penelope.

To be fair, he wasn't sure what made a painting good.

But he reasoned it had something to do with the way a painting could make someone feel. Could make someone see.

And when he looked at that painting, the painting Hannah had given him, he felt something. He saw what she saw.

He saw her. As she had been the day they met. He saw her searching. Her wondering.

And her loneliness.

One day, he mentioned the painting to his boss.

His boss was a man who had come from a faraway big city. He was a man with many degrees that taught him how to evaluate paintings. Being around him made Theodore nervous, his words garbled, feeling like spiky ice cubes in his mouth.

But he pushed through the ice-cube feeling. And he got his words out.

"I have a beautiful painting. You should see it."

The boss seemed unsure. Yet when Theodore placed the painting in front of him, he immediately saw it.

Hannah. Her searching. Her wondering. Her loneliness.

"Who is the girl?" his boss asked.

Theodore stared at the painting. He had looked at it so many times. And there were so many ways he could've answered that question. But because he missed Hannah, he said, "A mystery."

"Fantastic. All great art is a mystery waiting to be solved," his boss replied.

The boss offered to purchase the painting. The Penelope L. Brooks Museum wanted to add the painting to its permanent collection.

Theodore wasn't sure what to do. He loved the painting. He loved even more that Hannah had given him the painting. But this seemed like a chance to make Hannah's dream come true. Didn't she want other people to see her? To see what she had made? Didn't she want others to revel in her great mystery?

Ultimately, he agreed to his boss's offer. He eagerly called Hannah on the phone. Breathlessly, he told her the news.

"They've bought it!" he told her. "It's going to be on display for everyone to see. Can you believe it? Your art in a real museum. You'll have to come home and see it."

There was a long silence. It was the bone-chilling kind. Theodore immediately knew something was wrong.

"Hannah?"

"I gave it to you, Teddy. I gave *you* that painting. And you just gave it away."

She hung up.

Theodore figured she would call back. That she would adjust to the idea. That she would at least brighten when she opened the check from the museum that he sent her.

(He sent her all the money.)

She did not brighten. She sent the money back, envelope unopened.

Theodore never cashed the check. If Rami or Veda had explored his apartment that night, they would've found the check, neatly tucked in his nightstand. Still not deposited.

He waited for Hannah to call.

She didn't.

He waited. And waited.

He watched as more of her paintings popped up in museums around the country. Once, he drove to Chicago to see one of her paintings. When he stood in front of it, he could almost feel her there.

He reveled in the mystery of it. But as always, he saw her searching. Her wondering. Her loneliness.

The paintings weren't Hannah, though.

He kept his job at the Penelope. It made him sad to be so close to that painting every day. But it made him even sadder to imagine being far away from that painting. Sadness, he learned, was not a feeling you could outrun. Like a tide, it might ebb and flow, but it was always there.

Theodore hadn't heard from Hannah for years. Not a phone call. Not a letter.

Until one day, his phone rang. And it was Evergreen Pines, alerting him that Hannah had slipped into a coma.

Hannah had listed him as her emergency contact.

Theodore took this as a sign.

This was his chance to make things right. This was his chance to help her remember.

35

Remembering

Veda's eyes were wide. She and Rami were squeezed together in the back seat of Theodore's car. It was a small hatchback. Theodore barely fit in the front seat; his knees were crunched up, butting against the steering wheel. But like his apartment, the car was immaculately clean.

The cleanliness gave Rami another thought.

"It wasn't a mistake," Rami said. "You didn't toss that receipt away carelessly. You purposefully left it near the top of the dumpster, hoping someone would find it. You wanted to get caught."

Theodore's hands tightened on the steering wheel, his knuckles whitening. "I. Did. Not. Want. To. Get. Caught."

"But—" Rami protested.

"I can't believe that's your main takeaway from

what he just told us," Veda said. Her eyes were still wide like saucers. "What you did was so romantic, Theodore. You must really love Hannah."

Theodore made a scoffing sound. But it wasn't necessarily a disagreement.

Rami adjusted his seat belt and leaned forward. "You wanted the receipt to be found, though. If you hadn't, you wouldn't have just left it lying there, right on the top of the trash. Also, I had originally thought the receipt couldn't belong to you because of the time stamp. Did you not work that day?"

"I got Ed to cover my shift," Theodore said in a clipped, tight voice. The car was moving fast. As they approached the stop sign, Theodore slammed on the brakes. Rami and Veda jostled around in the back seat.

"Whoa," Veda said. "Who taught you to drive?"

Another scoff.

"But you wanted someone to find the receipt, right?" Rami pressed.

"I suppose that's true," Theodore said slowly while accelerating the car quickly. "I don't know. Who knows why people do what they do."

"So, you stole the painting during the deep clean," Rami pressed.

"Yes. It's clearly the best time to steal a painting if you're going to steal one," Theodore answered.

"Obviously," Veda said. She had a big smile on her face. Rami thought she maybe seemed all too happy to be hearing about a crime.

"You turned off the cameras," Rami said. "And you deleted footage."

"Easy enough," Theodore said. "I had to delete the footage of me. If someone saw me in the museum that day, everyone would've been suspicious."

"But how did you get around Ed?" Rami asked.

"Oh, that was easy, too. Old Ed is very predictable. He's taken the same break schedule for years. So that's what I did. I turned off the cameras, deleted the footage, and grabbed the painting while he was on break. I just walked out with it. Can you believe it? I walked out with the painting while Ed was watching basketball on his phone!"

Veda kept smiling. "And to think, I once thought the painting was stolen by a rich guy."

"Wait. I thought you said that was your theory you only shared with unserious people," Rami said.

"It was still a theory," Veda said, shrugging.

"I told you," Rami said. "Rich guys don't need to steal paintings. They can buy them."

"Ah. I think rich guys do often steal paintings. But this time it wasn't a rich guy. It was a . . ." Theodore parked the car. He got out and stretched.

"It was a romantic guy," Veda said.

"I don't know how romantic theft is," Rami whispered to her.

"I can hear you," Theodore said. "I have excellent hearing. Which, as I'm sure you could guess, comes in quite handy as a security guard."

"Sorry," Rami mumbled. "But I think I have a valid point."

"I still think it's romantic," Veda said. "We're here to see the ghost of your childhood best friend who you care so much about that you robbed an art museum for her! That's VERY romantic."

"Hannah's not a ghost," Theodore said sharply. "She's not dead. At least not yet."

Veda exchanged a concerned look with Rami. Rami shrugged.

The outside lights of the Penelope flickered on when they walked past, illuminating the expansive front porch and rounded front door.

"Are those lights on a timer or is someone here?" Veda whispered.

"You don't have to whisper. If someone's here, they're already watching us on camera," Theodore said.

Rami fought back a swallow. "Well, is someone here?"

"Someone is here," a voice answered. It was Ed. He opened the front door of the Penelope and peered out at them.

"Well, well," Ed said. "I knew you had something to do with this nonsense." He pointed at Rami.

"He actually doesn't," Theodore said.

"And I don't, either," Veda said, raising her hand. "I'm here, yes. But I'm not responsible for the missing painting. In case you're taking notes."

Ed scowled. "I'm not taking notes."

"Shouldn't you be, though?" Veda said, and Ed's scowl deepened. She shrugged sheepishly. "Sorry. Just a suggestion."

Ed turned toward Theodore. "Theodore, what are you doing here?"

Theodore sighed. He ran his hand over his nearly bald head. "I'll explain everything soon. And I'll return the painting."

Ed's eyes widened with so much surprise they looked like they were about to pop out of his face.

"Yeah, yeah," Theodore said. "It was me. But in order for me to return it, I need you to do one thing."

Ed looked dizzy. And a little confused. "I don't understand."

"Let us in the museum," Theodore said.

Ed shook his head. "You know I can't do that,

Theo. I need to call Dr. Hale right now. The police. You know I have to."

Theodore climbed up another step. "Do you want your painting back or not?"

"What do you want to do in there?" Ed asked. He still looked pretty dizzy.

"I can answer that," Veda said, raising her hand again. "We want to—"

"If you want me to return the painting safe and sound, let us in. It'll only take five minutes," Theo said.

"Um, it might take a little longer depending on how long it takes to find her," Rami offered, surprised by the sound of his own voice.

Ed's gaze shot in Rami's direction. "Find who?"

Theodore waved his hand in the air. "Never mind about that. Are you going to let us in or not?"

There was a long pause. "Okay," Ed said. "You can walk in, but I'm calling the police immediately. Do you understand?"

None of them answered. They walked right in.

"I seriously am," Ed called out. "I'm calling the police. And the cameras are on this time!"

In Which Blue Remembers Who She Is

It didn't end up taking long for them to find her.

The girl was waiting for them in Cherry Hall. Just like Rami hoped she would be.

"Blue," Rami said. "We've figured out who you are."

Blue turned to Rami. She floated toward him. "You're back."

"Holy cow," Theodore said. He stumbled backward.

"We told you," Veda said.

"It's you again," Blue said.

"Impossible," Theodore whispered. His whole face was pale.

"You look like you've seen a ghost," Veda said.

"Veda," Rami hissed.

Veda shrugged. "What? It's funny."

Rami smiled despite himself. She was right. It was kind of funny.

"You've been ignoring me," Blue said. "But I know that I know you. Somehow. Right? The turtle knows, too. She drew you. Or she tried to draw you. She is a turtle, after all."

"I knew it!" Veda made a pumping motion with her arm. "Didn't I tell you the turtle is the one who drew his face?"

Rami made a face. He wasn't quite ready to believe in a drawing turtle.

Blue nodded. "It was the turtle. She really did a remarkable job. Quite impressive."

Blue kept staring at Theodore, who, maybe because of her staring, kept backing up until he'd reached the wall. His shoulder brushed against the frame of the sailboat painting.

"Ed won't want you to touch that painting," Rami offered. He gestured at the ceiling. "And we're on camera."

Theodore shot him a look, and Rami gave him an apologetic shrug.

"Are you going to tell me who you are?" Blue said. "I'm sorry to be rude, but I have no idea who I am. Let alone who anyone else is."

Theodore looked at Blue. He looked at Rami and Veda. "I can't believe what I'm seeing. How is this possible? She's really here?"

"She's really here," Veda said.

Blue floated closer to Theodore. At first, Rami thought Theodore was wincing. But as he studied his face some more, he saw that although Theodore's eyes were glossy with tears, they were shining.

"Hannah," Theodore whispered. "It's me. Theodore."

Something flickered across Blue's face. Recognition maybe. Perhaps relief.

"Hannah," she repeated. She tilted her head to look down at her floating feet. She craned her neck to look up at the museum ceiling. Her eyes darted around the room.

And then she vanished.

But as Rami looked around the room, searching for Blue, he realized that for the first time in a long time, he wasn't alone.

37 The Story

So I'm going to tell you the story now. The way I heard it.

Here's how it goes:

Back at Evergreen Pines at exactly 2:41 in the morning, Hannah Frances Bottemtow miraculously awoke from her coma.

Hannah Frances Bottemtow blinked her eyes open. She gasped for air.

And she said, "Theodore."

Soon after, a man appeared at the doorway of her room, which was crowded with nurses.

I bet you can guess who this man is.

The man was in possession of a painting. A painting that she had created. A painting that was missing and wanted by the authorities.

It is said that Hannah Frances Bottemtow sat up

in bed. That she took the painting from Theodore's hands. That despite protests in the room, she took the painting out of its frame. That she reached for a medical tool. And with that tool, she peeled back the canvas to reveal another painting.

This painting was a lot like the first one.

Except, in this painting, the girl was not alone.

In this painting, there was the girl from the first painting. There was the apple tree. But there was also a boy. And the boy?

The boy was looking at the girl.

And the girl was looking at the boy.

If you visit the Penelope L. Brooks Museum today, you will only find one of these paintings on display.

It is the one with the girl and the boy.

It is not *Untitled*.

It is called *Look*.

There is a plaque that hangs in the museum that explains the story of how *Look* was discovered. It explains about *Untitled* and how it went missing, and how it was recovered. Several names that you will now recognize are mentioned on the plaque.

Much to Rami's delight, many people actually do read this plaque.

There is a lot of interest in a painting that once

went missing. But there is even more interest in the painting that was amazingly discovered behind the painting that went missing.

Most of all, there is continual interest in the story of how the missing painting was found. And how the new painting was discovered behind it. It is a story that keeps people coming back.

It is a story that sells tickets to the museum.

The plaque tells some of the story. But not all of it. That's because only a few people know about Blue and Agatha. Only a few people know about the marks Rami saw on the wall of Cherry Hall.

But now you know about those things.

Why No One Ended Up in Jail in Their Pajamas

The painting that was known as *Untitled* now hangs in Theodore D. Cornell's apartment. It was proven that the painting always belonged to him, and not the museum, as the check to purchase the payment never cleared.

No one was ever apprehended in the case now known as the Strange Thing That Happened in Cherry Hall at the Penelope L. Brooks Museum.

The details of why were mostly kept from the public.

But ultimately it was decided that you could not prosecute someone for taking an object that legally belonged to them.

Plus, the real truth is Dr. Hale decided that *Look* was going to sell so many admission tickets she was willing to excuse Theodore's actions.

Rami and Veda were celebrated for their role in helping to recover the painting. But they were also grounded by their parents.

But once their respective groundings were over, Veda and Rami met every week after school at the library. Rami still went with his mom to work sometimes, but it was nice to have another place to go.

It was nice to have someone else to be with.

It was nice to not feel so alone anymore.

Theodore D. Cornell's Apartment

I should tell you, too, that Theodore D. Cornell's apartment is no longer just Theodore D. Cornell's apartment.

Someone else lives there with him.

Someone he sometimes calls Blue.

Asking

Rami wasn't quite sure how to start, but he knew what he had to do.

He took the Photo out from under his bed. He looked at it again. He ran his fingers over the man's mustache. He studied his mom's wide smile.

And then he walked into the kitchen. He set the Photo down on the table.

"Mom," he said.

"Rami?" she answered.

For a second, Rami didn't say anything.

She walked over to him. She looked at the Photo. "Oh, Rami," she said. She reached out and squeezed his hand. "Let's talk, okay?"

Rami nodded. He squeezed his mom's hand back. He looked at the surprise bird painting on the wall. He found the beak. And then the talons.

And finally, the wings.

"I have a lot of questions," he said. "And I also need to tell you some stuff."

Rami had learned recently that sometimes it was hardest to see what was right in front of you. And sometimes it was hardest to say the things that were most obvious.

But he was going to try.

He didn't swallow. He kept talking.

Where Is Our Turtle?

It is said that Agatha still lives in the courtyard behind the museum.

She is still drawing.

Sometimes people notice; sometimes they don't.

You'll have to let me know if you ever make it to the Penelope L. Brooks Museum to visit.

You'll have to let me know what you see.

ACKNOWLEDGMENTS

Enormous thanks to:

My wonderful agent, Brenda Bowen, and the whole team at the Book Group.

Alessandra Balzer, for helping to shepherd and guide this book with her warm and sharp and brilliant eye and for embracing Agatha immediately. Thank you for always helping me figure out the story I want to tell and for leading the way through all the bumps and curves of the creative process.

Rich Thomas, for his fantastic insights and enthusiasm—I appreciate it so much! The entire incredible team at Harper Children's—Liate Stehlik, Kathy Faber, Kerry Moynagh, Nellie Kurtzman, Lisa Disarro, Patty Rosati, Taylan Salvati, Robby Imfeld, Stephanie Macy, Mimi Rankin, Christina Carpino, Sabrina Abballe, Nicole Wills, Caitlin Lonning, Mikayla Lawrence, Paige Pagan, Julia Tyler, Jenna Stempel-Lobell, and Alison Donalty. Thank you for everything you do for my books. I'm very grateful.

Matt Rockefeller, for the beautiful cover and gorgeous interior illustrations.

Every librarian, bookseller, and educator who has uplifted and shared my work. Thank you for everything you do to get books in the hands of young people who need them.

All my friends—I am beyond lucky that there are too many of you to name, but while writing books can be a lonely endeavor, your support and companionship inspire and fortify me. I appreciate you all.

Tae Keller, John Schu, James Ponti, and Karina Yan Glaser, for reading the book early and responding with such kindness and excitement.

My family, for all your support and love. Greg, Lillian, and Juniper—you are always my favorite part of the story. I see you and thank you for seeing me.